The Hungry Writer is a simmered reduction of five years of 'the hungry writer' blog by award-winning writer and lyrical lover of food, Lynne Rees. Stories, poems, childhood memories, personal recipes, and 365 Hungry Writing Prompts. Eat, Live, Write.

Lynne Rees was born and grew up in Port Talbot, South Wales but left in 1978 to work in offshore banking in Jersey, Channel Islands. She moved to Kent in 1985 where, for twelve years, she ran her own second-hand and antiquarian bookshop, Foxed & Bound (the inspiration for her novel, *The Oven House*).

She began writing in 1988 after discovering Natalie Goldberg's book, *Writing Down the Bones*, studied for her Master's degree in writing with the University of Glamorgan between 1994 and 1996 (with the celebrated Welsh poet, Gillian Clarke) and was awarded an International Hawthornden Writers' Fellowship in 2003.

She has lived in Florida, Barcelona and, between 2007 and 2011, in Antibes in the South of France, where she renovated an early 20th century Maison de Maître just 200 metres from the Cap d'Antibes and the Mediterranean shoreline. She currently lives in Kent, with her husband, the artist, Tony Crosse, in a house at the edge of their working apple orchard not far from the North Downs, and works as a freelance writer, editor and writing coach.

You can keep up to date with the hungry writer's food-biased life at www.lynnerees.com

Taste, scent, memories and recipes melt into a glorious blend of food, from the South of France to her native Wales and Kent, life-enhancing vignettes about cooking and looking at the world – and practical advice about learning to write as well as she does. Lynne Rees has served up a sumptuous feast for mind, body and soul.

Deborah Lawrenson, bestselling author of
The Lantern and *The Sea Garden*

The life of a hungry writer is a life of craving, reflection and deep engagement, and *The Hungry Writer* captures all aspects of that rich way of being. The book tells multiple and interconnected stories: of sources of inspiration and a commitment to inspiring others; of sourcing food and the joy of feeding others; and of the three big themes: love and loss and home. And all told with a passion for words and writing, and a profoundly moving generosity of spirit.

Shaun Levin, creator of
The Writing Notebooks

Authors who love eating as much as writing know that words have flavour and provide sustenance, and that a good read is a satisfying meal for the soul. In this sense, Lynne Rees is a chef, and *The Hungry Writer* is a feast.

Suzan Colón, author of
*Cherries in Winter: My Family's Recipe
for Hope in Hard Times*

So it happens that when I really write of hunger, I am really writing about love and the hunger for it, and warmth and the love of it and the hunger for it ... and then the warmth and richness and fine reality of hunger satisfied ... and it is all one.

M.F.K. Fisher, *The Art of Eating*

One cannot think well, love well, sleep well, if one has not dined well.

Virginia Woolf, *A Room of One's Own*

the hungry writer

Lynne Rees

Other books by the author

Real Port Talbot (Seren, 2013)
forgiving the rain (Snapshot Press, 2012)
Another Country, Haiku Poetry from Wales (as Editor) (Gomer, 2011)
Messages (with Sarah Salway) 2nd edition (bluechrome, 2008)
Learning How to Fall (Parthian, 2005)
The Oven House (bluechrome, 2004)

the hungry writer

Writing
prompts

Recipes

Stories

Lynne Rees

For Rosie — stay hungry for
everything! lae
Lynne

Cultured Llama Publishing

First published in 2015 by
Cultured Llama Publishing
11 London Road
Teynham, Sittingbourne
ME9 9QW
www.culturedllama.co.uk

A CIP record for this book is available from The British Library

ISBN 978-0-9932119-3-5

Printed in Great Britain by Lightning Source UK Ltd

Typographical design by Bob Carling

Cover design by Tony Crosse

Contents

The Beginning

While I was teaching creative writing, at the University of Kent, a couple of students commented that I couldn't get through a seminar without mentioning food or drink. Really? I didn't set out with that intention. There were no explicit teaching points about food in my lesson plans. But, yes, they were right. A bruise could be the colour of raw liver; the scent of bread heavy with promise. And, of course, if I was teaching on or around 1st March – St David's Day, the patron saint of Wales – whichever writing groups I was leading that week enjoyed my buttery home-made Welshcakes.

And there was more food. More than I realised.

Food played a prominent part in my first book, a novel called *The Oven House* – it symbolised comfort and nurture, attempted to soothe the desolate landscape of lost love through the cherishing intensities of heat and taste. It is sprinkled, literally and metaphorically, through my poetry too: an unsettling chip shop owner, a bare-breasted woman striding past a grocery store, tomatoes, milk, bread, chestnuts, olives, eggs, a single golden apple. And since 2010 it has been the central ingredient in the hungry writer's weekly blog, a place where I eventually settled to record the moments where food, words and life collide.

Molly Wizenberg, in *A Homemade Life: Stories and Recipes from My Kitchen Table*, says, 'Food is never just food. It's also a way of getting at something else: who we are, who we have been, and who we want to be.' The ideas of 'who I am' and 'who I've been' were certainly on my mind when I moved to the South of France in 2008, a thousand miles away from friends and family in England and Wales. Perhaps it was this geographical distance that generated an intimacy with my past and propelled me towards writing more directly about my life, about the place where I was born, about my parents, the houses and kitchens I lived in and visited, about the child I was and the children who came into my life. About loss and discovery, about home and what the word meant to me. And about leaving home and finding ways back. And how could I write about all that without writing about food? The food I grew up with and the food I learned to eat and cook.

It took a little while, and a couple of false starts, but in October 2010 'the hungry writer' blogged for the first time.

I set out on that journey with no precise destination in mind, just with an intention to ensure that food, life and writing were the principal ingredients of each blog-post, and with a personal commitment to blog every week without fail. If I could be disciplined enough to keep it up then it might prove that what I had to say really mattered to me. And if it mattered to me perhaps it would matter to other people too.

The blog posts varied from week to week: childhood memories, stories about holidays and lost friends, places, glimpses into history, elegies and complaints. Some weeks what I wanted to say was already there at my fingertips, words and memories spilling onto the screen. Other weeks I found myself slouching towards my Wednesday deadline with an empty cupboard, bereft of ideas, or starting and abandoning them: frustrated, disappointed, doubtful. But I'd made myself that promise. So I pushed on: I wrote through the doubts. And that commitment to the process of writing inevitably surprised me with the unexpected, the blossoming of an idea I hadn't previously considered or even a memory that had remained dormant for years but was now front seat and waving at me.

I did not have a childhood informed by adventures in food. I was born and grew up on a large council estate in South Wales. Dad worked shifts at the local steelworks. Mam was a housewife looking after three children. We ate cereal or toast and jam (Robertson's Bramble Seedless was my favourite) for breakfast; meat or fish with potatoes and vegetables for dinner in the middle of the day; sandwiches or baked beans for tea when we came home from school.

Dad's shifts meant he mostly ate with us on Sundays, if it was his day off: thinly sliced roast topside of beef, or a leg of lamb, and the occasional chicken in the days before factory farming made them a cheap meal. I used to help with gravy making (the laborious stirring over a low heat until it started to boil and thicken), mixing the batter for Yorkshire puddings, and chopping garden mint with sugar for a vinegary mint sauce. When he was working nights, Dad ate off a stool in front of the television around 8pm, or in the middle of the afternoon after a morning shift. Sometimes it was a dinner Mam had saved, from earlier or the day before, and warmed up over a saucepan of steam. Occasionally it was a Vesta Beef Curry and Rice – that exotic single box of 1960's rice and dehydrated curry sauce bought especially for him, which he allowed us to taste.

I remember take-away fishcake and chips at the end of a long day of family visits in West Wales. I remember the regimented meals at a Butlin's holiday camp in the mid-1960s. I remember my first boyfriend, a sophisticated 24-year-old, taking me to an Italian restaurant in Swansea where I ate Veal Marsala and sat in awe of a bottle of straw-covered Chianti.

But it was only after I left home in 1978, transferred by the Midland Bank to their offshore offices in Jersey, in the Channel Islands, that food metamorphosed into something more than ingredients presented to me on a plate. There I was surrounded by French, Italian & Portuguese cooking – from haute cuisine to easy-going bistro – prepared, ordered and eaten by people who loved food, who relished fresh ingredients and menus in the same way I relished opening one of my monthly book club novels. My managers, a conflagration of boyfriends, the bank's customers who took me out for lunch or dinner, kindly restaurateurs, and, at home, Robert Carrier's inspiring, but grindingly effortful, weekly cookery magazines all taught me about good food and wine, and with occasionally embarrassing learning curves. Who knew that plates were deliberately tilted on the downturned tines of a fork so melted butter pooled around the fat tips of new season asparagus and that a head waiter would correct you when you took the fork away? You did? Well this was 1981. At that point I'd never met an asparagus. Not to mention asparagus serving tongs!

The hungry writer blog had its fifth anniversary this year: memories, stories, reflections, restaurant successes and failures, mine and other people's recipes, and the lightly fleshed bones of a few books that have entertained, inspired and intrigued me have all featured from week to week. But the unwavering weekly component has been the writing prompts. I have offered them without comment or instruction in every single blog-post, to other writers – apprentice, emerging and established – who want to exercise their creative minds, follow their thoughts freely across a page or screen and see where they lead. I know from my own experience of workshops and writing groups that spontaneous writing sometimes delivers me to a place that crackles with life and flavour. Other times the writing feels flat and disappointing, like dough that has failed to rise. But I also know that regular writing practice pays off: we can discover what we want to write through writing. And the hungry writer blog is proof of that.

In 2012 a collection of some of the more lyrical posts from that first year, shaped and seasoned with haiku poetry, were published in *forgiving the rain*, a fragmented memoir on the theme of home, of leaving it and finding a way back.

And I am convinced I would not have been commissioned to write the upbeat and offbeat psycho-geographical account of my hometown in South Wales, *Real Port Talbot*, without those hungry writer years, the weeks and months of sieving words and phrases in an attempt to find a voice that felt expansively and authentically mine.

This book is a simmered reduction of the blog's first five years with an offering of sincere but amateur recipes and 365 writing prompts to keep you writing hungrily throughout one whole year. In an attempt to create some semblance of order, out of an inevitably eclectic blog written in the moment, I begin in Antibes, France, at Villa les Marronniers, the house my husband, Tony, and I bought and renovated between 2007 and 2011, and where the hungry writer recorded her first words in 2010. And I end in Kent, at The Applehouse, our home set amongst 20 acres of apple trees, and where I still live. The pages between those two markers are a bit like letters from the emotional and physical landscapes of my life: memories, holidays, family visits to Wales, and reflections on the ordinariness of my day to day life. There are tears and laughter, love and loss, some clarity and confusion, all of which I hope will trigger your own memories, ideas and explorations.

But please understand you do not have to be a food lover to use and enjoy the book. Food has taken me deeper into my life, made me question what I thought I knew, led me to this place, but your own guides and muses are likely to have different guises. Let the stories and writing prompts lead you to words that will help identify your own story makers. Music, perhaps. Or shoes, park benches, beaches, birdsong.

At the back of the book you'll find 'Ideas for Readers, Writers and Writing Groups' with suggestions for using the writing prompts and discussing the work produced in a more structured setting, but they can also work for regular private practice or just be dipped into at random, as and when the desire to write presents itself. Think of them as the writing equivalent of a morning coffee-break with your feet up, or afternoon tea with biscuits; a few minutes, or more, of playfulness; little imagination-igniters that have no expectations of you. But they might also surprise you when you feel a door opening on the unexpected. Acknowledge the quickened beat of your heart, the joy, the small pool of loss, or whatever emotion arises in you, and keep on writing. This is where the energy of your own work lies: when you feel it, when it brings you home to yourself.

Eat, live, write well.

Lynne
the hungry writer at lynnerees.com

Slow

One of the reasons I love our house in Antibes so much is that pretty much everything is within walking distance. The centre of Antibes is along the seafront and up the broad, plane tree-lined Boulevard Albert 1er: supermarkets, La Poste, our bank and insurance agent, the Mairie, the Provençal market, bakers and fishmongers, chocolate shops, and enough restaurants, bars and cafés to satisfy several years of hunger are all there. Juan les Pins lies in the opposite direction, a steady climb to the crest of Chemin de Sables from where, 75 years ago, the recently renovated 19th century palazzo must have had a sweeping and uncluttered view of the bay and the Cap d'Antibes. These days the horizon is mostly filled with high rise apartment blocks that start on land once belonging to the palazzo's estate and trickle down the hill to La Pinede at the edge of the town, a park full of umbrella pines, clumps of Strelitzia, or Birds of Paradise, and fairground rides for little children.

In my first few months of living here it took me ten minutes or less to reach the centre of Antibes. Two years later it's more like twenty. The heat, of course, is one reason to slow down. Even in February the sun can be hot enough to have you wiping perspiration from your forehead and tugging the damp cotton of your T-shirt away from your skin if you set out route-march style. Try that in July or August and you find yourself liquefying after the first 200 yards. But that's only part of it. The engine that drives life on the Côte d'Azur runs at a slower pace.

It might be easy shifting down a gear during a two week holiday but getting used to a slower pace every single day is more challenging. And even now I can still feel impatience growing in me like a puffball mushroom when the fishmonger or greengrocer keeps on chatting, at length and inconsequentially, with another customer regardless of how many people are waiting.

Yesterday, when I stopped to buy some Carpentras strawberries at the greengrocers, worth every cent of the 4,50 € for their sweetness and deep red hearts, the woman ignored me and carried on tidying up the punnets of soft fruit, shifting them towards the front of the stall. She eventually acknowledged me with a nod, but she didn't rush, and stood back to admire her handy work before stepping behind the stall to ask me, 'Qu'est-ce que vous voulez?' The strawberries that have been sitting in my hands for the last 4 minutes?!

Breathe now.

While she was wrapping the strawberries I tasted a little slice of melon from the sample plate (the first Provençal cantaloupes of the season) and told her I'd take one of those too. She picked up one, then another, weighed each one in her palm, tapped them and put them back. She took a third to the scale then changed her mind again, brought it back and exchanged it. 'Ça c'est un bon melon,' she said, and I had no doubt she was right.

I won't idealise France; it's not always the case that 'slow' is good. I signed a mandate for a new savings account at the bank two weeks ago and the account still hasn't been opened. But that's French bureaucracy for you; even the French complain of *la paperasse*, the bumf of paperwork and length of time that even the smallest administrative task can entail.

But sometimes slow is wonderful. No one has ever chosen a melon for me with such care. And not necessarily because she wanted to please or impress me, but because it was her *metier*, her trade, and doing it well was what mattered.

Hungry Writing Prompts 1 – 7

Write about walking away from home.

Write about what you can see on the horizon.

Write about slowing down.

Write about summer fruits.

Write about waiting.

Write about someone who cares.

Write about doing something well.

SLOW TOMATOES

What you need:
- ☐ Tomatoes
- ☐ Dried herbs
- ☐ Olive oil

What you do:
- ☐ Cut the tomatoes in half horizontally and place cut side up in a baking tray. Drizzle with olive oil and sprinkle with dried herbs – oregano, or Italian, or Herbes de Provence. If you're using winter or forced tomatoes you might want to add a little salt and sugar too, but don't over season as the flavour does intensify during the slow cooking
- ☐ Now you have a choice. Either put them in the oven at 100°C for 3 to 4 hours or at 50°C overnight. This timing is okay for medium to large tomatoes

They have a concentrated, mock-sun dried flavour when they cool, which is lovely with crusty bread. I've also used them in a tomato and sliced buffalo mozzarella starter, stacking them on top of each other and dressing them with roughly chopped basil and balsamic glaze.

Slow here means flavour. Means good.

Appropriation

My French friend, Kate, is telling me about a spat she had with a barman, at the swanky Les Belles Rives hotel in Juan les Pins. She'd walked away from her table to take a photograph, leaving her bag and drink there, and he'd run across to her waving *l'addition*, the bill.

'I thought this was a 5 star establishment,' she said. 'In a 5 star establishment the bill is always delivered to the table.' Kate is all of five foot tall, but she can wither someone who crosses her with her square shoulders and a dark-eyed glare in less than five seconds. The barman couldn't grovel an apology quickly enough.

It's a good story. But then she goes on.

'Did you imagine I would *filer à l'anglaise?*' she said to him.

Hang on. What's that?

The verb *filer* in French is multi-functional. It can mean 'to spin' (as in wool), 'to extend' (as in drawing out a sound, a note), 'to shadow' (as in Police), 'to veer out' (as in nautical), to go stringy (as in cheese), and to dash off. *Filer à l'anglaise* is supposed to mean 'to leave or go away, without notice or permission'. In Kate's story it meant 'doing a runner'!

I suppose it's all down to the good old *entente cordiale* that exists between the British and the French (when the French say *les anglais* they mean, for the most part, the British). We call them 'frogs'; they call us *les rosbifs*. Where we say 'a French letter', they say *une capote anglaise*. The one expression that we don't offer a British English equivalent for is the imaginative, *Les Anglais ont debarqué*. Literally, 'The English have landed', but metaphorically, 'I have my period'. It allegedly goes back to the Napoleonic wars and the redcoats of the English soldiers being easy to spot at a distance and the inevitable aftermath of combat. But in fairness to the French they're also happy to use their favourite aunt to express the same idea as in, *Ma tante Rose a débarqué*, so let's not take it personally.

Of course, there's also the delightful *un jardin à l'anglaise* – a landscaped garden. And the delicious *la crème anglaise*, thin pouring custard they float islands of fluffy meringue on, not as gloopy or startlingly yellow as a lot of English custard. And the pretty *les Anglaises* – ringlets.

But as an acknowledgement of traditionally strained Franco-British relations I have appropriated their classic Apple *Tarte Tatin* and made some of my own improvements.

PEAR TARTE TATIN

What you need:

- ☐ Ready-made puff pastry cut to fit the diameter of a shallow round dish that doesn't have fluted edges (this is important, as you'll see later)
- ☐ Depending on the size of your dish (and the size of your pears) about 6 to 8 pears. I use Williams or Comice
- ☐ 4 oz of unsalted butter
- ☐ 4 oz of soft light brown sugar
- ☐ 2 tablespoons of golden syrup

What you do:

- ☐ Slowly melt the butter with the sugar and golden syrup to make a thick caramel sauce. Be careful not to let it burn
- ☐ Peel and quarter the pears, slice out any core, and drop them in the caramel. Stir gently to coat them all and let them simmer gently for about 3 to 4 minutes until they just start to soften
- ☐ Take them off the heat, spoon out the fruit one by one and place them, round-side down, shoulder to shoulder, in the dish. Pack in as many as you can. Pour the caramel sauce into a jug – you can heat it up later in the microwave to make it go liquidy again
- ☐ Place the pastry round on top of the pears and press down lightly so you can make out the pear shapes under it, like puppies under a blanket. The edge of the pastry will look a little wavy
- ☐ Cook for between 25 to 35 minutes at 200°C until the pastry is golden
- ☐ Let the tart cool for about 15 mins then, making sure that no edges of pastry have stuck to the dish (loosen it with the tip of a sharp knife if it has), place a big flat plate over the dish and flip it over quickly. This is the point when the flat-edged dish, not the fluted edge, is crucial. The first time I made this in a dish with a fluted edge hot caramel sauce flicked out all over me. Painful. But delicious!
- ☐ Heat up the caramel sauce and trickle it over the tart or serve in a jug on the side. *Et voilà!* Lovely with *crème fraiche*, ice-cream but also surprisingly good with a slice of firm cheese: Manchego, Comté or good old reliable Cheddar

Hungry Writing Prompts 8 – 14

Write about drinking in a hotel bar.

Write about running after someone.

Write about being misunderstood.

Write about doing something without permission.

Write about a time when *Les Anglais ont debarqué*.

Write about a garden.

Write about the colour yellow.

Becoming More

I t is a truth acknowledged by my family and close friends that I am not equipped with the maternal gene. I never wanted my own children and as the years have passed I've remained content with my childless existence. I'm particularly twitchy around babies, or to be more precise, their general messiness. Apart from holding new born family members and writing a poem to celebrate their arrival into the world I've managed to keep a distance from the whole birthing, feeding, nappy-changing, crying and vomiting side of life.

The first time I looked after my step-granddaughter, Summer, she was a few months past her third birthday. Her mother, Tony's eldest daughter, had a hectic week of OFSTED inspections at her North London school so could we please have Summer to stay at our house in Kent? Just for the week: she'd drop her off on Sunday and pick her up on Friday. Please?

Okay, Summer was, mercifully, well beyond the nappy stage, but the idea of being responsible for a young child for five whole days filled me with dread. Not just the responsibility of mealtimes and bath-times and bedtimes, and 'Do you want to wee?' and 'Don't touch that!', but the anticipated boredom too.

At the end of that week I wrote my first poem for her:

Awakening

When the child comes, she rouses them,
all the never-borns, the never-will-be-borns
I never missed or wanted:
busy feet tamp across wooden boards,
scurries of handprints challenge the walls,

and I move in patterns I haven't known –
trapping her weight against my hip,
remembering not to heat her plate,
side-stepping with precision
a torn McDonald's crown,
a bear's sweater discarded on the stairs.

Her hand's a small island
on the flesh of my face. Her heat
creeps through my skin when I comfort her
in the hours before dawn.

The first night the house is empty of her
I start awake to a muster of footsteps
outside my door, cries.

It is not only blood that binds us to one another. But how to articulate what it is? That connection we can suddenly make with people of any age?

I don't believe it was solely her vulnerability, or my responsibility for her safety, or her dependence on me, although they all must have played some part in my emotional response. It felt more like something shared. She added a dimension to my life. My life expanded because I got to know her.

'Who are you?' she asked my reflection one day when she was about five as we stood in front of the bathroom mirror cleaning our teeth.
'What do you mean?'
'Well, you're not my nanny.'
'Strictly speaking, no.'
'And you're not my aunty.'

'No.'
'So who are you?'
'Who do you think I am?' I asked her.
She stared into the mirror again.
'I think you're my best friend,' she said.

This morning, in my kitchen in France, she is making chocolate fridge cake with me.

Before she arrived I was a little uneasy about what to expect. She turned 16 last month, and I also lack another gene that enables me to understand and endure the unpredictability of teenagers. And with me living in France and her at boarding school in the UK we haven't spent any real time with each other during the last couple of years.

And there have been a few moments during the last week when I have felt as if I am getting to know her all over again: as she tests out different identities, strikes a pose, as moods slip through her. But all these things seem incidental to the person she is at her core, the core that still reveals itself in her smile, the way she still hugs me as tight as a glove, reminders of who she was already becoming at the age of three.

Hungry Writing Prompts 15 - 21

Write about a baby.

Write about your responsibilities.

Write about feeling vulnerable.

Write about your reflection in the mirror.

Write about your different roles and identities.

Write about what expands your life.

Write about a best friend.

Pantry

M y favourite room in Villa les Marronniers is the pantry or *garde-manger*. A pantry is something I've wanted in a house for a long time. A proper pantry, a little room you can walk into, not just a larder cupboard.

You see the windows at the back? They don't have any glass, just fine mosquito mesh to keep out insects and let in the cool air from under the terrace outside. To be honest, during the summer there's not a great deal of difference between the temperature in the pantry and the temperature in the kitchen, but in autumn, winter and spring you can feel the cool, or even cold, rush of air when you open the door.

The word 'pantry' has its roots in the late Latin, *panarius*, bread-seller, from *panis*, bread, and rose up to greet us in English through the old French *paneterie*, from *panetier*, baker.

There is something floury and sweet about pantries. Perhaps the sound of the word itself triggers a connection to 'pastries'. The smell in my granny's pantry in Llanelli, in West Wales, was like crumbs from yesterday's bread mixed with the scent of condensed milk.

I only have a single memory of the pantry in the house where I was born. It might have had a yellow door. I am sure there was an air-brick in the outside wall for ventilation.

Summer of '63

We were the first people at our end of Chrome Avenue to have a fridge. Preparation for it had started weeks before – the brick pantry in the corner of the kitchen was knocked down, new lino laid on the floor. When it was delivered, the neighbours came out to watch its white bulk being trolleyed through the back gate. The next day my mother made ice-lollies from orange squash and I sucked mine until my gums ached.

I was playing in the sandpit in the garden when I told my friend Kathryn about our new fridge. She hit me over the head with a long-handled spade and ran home crying. My mother said Kathryn didn't like me being different from her. And we were different now. Our butter was hard. We had frozen peas.

I have a love-spoon on the pantry door. These carved wooden spoons are now a craft tradition in Wales, but they were originally made and presented by young men to convey their romantic intent. I bought this one for Tony, shortly after we met in 1985, and it's travelled with us from house to house, from country to country. The symbols are universal: two interlinking hearts, a wheel.

And the pantry door feels like the right place for it. It reminds me, before I even begin to cook, that food I prepare without love, or prepare impatiently or even resentfully, generally ends up, at best, mediocre, at worst, inedible.

Hungry Writing Prompts 22 – 28

Write about opening a cupboard door.

Write about a room that has a particular smell.

Write about what's changed.

Write about ice.

Write about something given with love.

Write about your heart.

Write about not eating.

Home to Home

The last thing my dad says to me before I leave for the train station is, 'The house comes alive when you're home.' And then I'm in the taxi, driving away in the rain, watching my parents waving from the porch window.

I cannot think of my dad without thinking of his garden in Port Talbot, South Wales, which he has brought to life every year for nearly 60 years with potatoes, beans, carrots, beetroot, onions, sweetcorn, cabbage. I see him digging, planting, thinning out, or bending over a row of plump onions, twisting down their tops to allow the bulbs to dry. The coalbunker in the garden was demolished nearly 50 years ago, but in my imagination I smell onions inside its dark walls, strung into plaits and hung in the cool amongst his forks, hoes and spades.

Snow along the tracks as my train passes through Bridgend, Cardiff, Newport where I change for Bristol, then take a bus to the airport for my flight back to Nice.

I remember the winter of 1962/63, the winter Sylvia Plath died in London, the one people still talk about along with 1947, and now, perhaps, 2010 with its airport closures and blocked motorways. I remember staring out of the front-room window at the snow lying thickly along Chrome Avenue, hiding all the pavements and gardens, and continuing to fall, in big, slow flakes. I am 4 years old, wearing a white tartan skirt, standing on the sofa, my fingertips pressing into the claret-coloured Rexine. But if this is a true memory why do I see myself from behind? Why don't I see only the street, the view through the window? How much of my past is invented, a patchwork of memory and imagination?

Tony asked me to marry him on a flight from Heathrow to Miami in September 2007. He stood up in front of our bulkhead seats and said, 'Blods (his nickname for me), will you dance with me?' There's not a lot of room in a bulkhead so it was more swaying back and forth on the same spot than dancing. And then he asked. And I said yes.

We didn't want to get married. We'd lived together since 1985. In fact, ever since we first discussed it, I couldn't stop thinking about stories of people who'd lived quite happily together for twenty plus years before suddenly deciding to get married, and how they'd split up within a year. But it was so much easier to buy the house in Antibes as a married couple rather than a co-habiting one; French property laws are complex and inheritance tax between 'unrelated' people is cripplingly high.

And because it was purely an administrative choice for us we didn't want to mark the day in any way. We didn't want to suggest to anyone, and particularly to ourselves, that things would be different from now on. So getting married in South Florida while we were there on holiday seemed the easiest and most 'non-markable' thing to do.

But you have photographs? people ask. No, sorry. We didn't do that either. But we did laugh in Deerfield Beach Town Hall with a Public Notary who looked like Whoopi Goldberg and who squealed, 'You guys!' each time she asked about friends, witnesses, cameras, flowers etc. After 30 minutes and a bill for $135 we went back to the little bungalow we'd rented on Hillsboro Beach, had pancakes for brunch and then went for a swim.

That was over three years ago. Now here he is, waiting for me on the other side of the Plexi-glass security screen when I come through Passport Control at Nice. He jumps up and down and waves with both hands, mouthing 'Helloooo,' oblivious to people standing around him. If he asked me to dance now, even with the screen between us, I'd say yes.

Hungry Writing Prompts 29 – 35

Write about something your father said.

Write about waving goodbye.

Write about looking out of a train window.

Write about snow.

Write about a proposal of marriage.

Write about something done out of necessity.

Write about dancing.

Saying Sorry with Tapenade

an icicle melts
in my mitten
I say I'm sorry

I wrote the above haiku as part of a text for a children's picture book, *tiny shivers*. The images of cold resistance and a gradual, but not necessarily comfortable, yielding captures the way I felt as a child when I knew I'd done something wrong, had behaved badly, and was expected to apologise. I think it still captures how I feel as an adult.

I'm probably not alone in finding it difficult to admit I was wrong about something. I have an automatic defensive reaction that propels me to point out, with sound reasons and logic of course, what the other person didn't understand, how they might have misinterpreted my words, my actions.

But underneath my clear sense of righteousness there's a physical tension in the place just below my collar-bone, and even more strongly in my solar-plexus, which I'm pretty sure represents my stubborn little ego not wanting to humble itself. Because saying sorry, really saying sorry properly and meaning it, takes a lot of humility.

Why is it so difficult? Are we born with the desire to protect ourselves and see apologising as tantamount to admitting weakness, as having to relinquish personal power to someone else? Is there a way we can teach kids how to make apologies with a positive frame of mind so it feels easier, and just and right, in that moment as well as later in life?

If you grew up in the 60s and early 70s you'd have seen the film *Love Story* and will remember Ryan O'Neal saying to Ali McGraw, 'Love means never having to say you're sorry'. It's one of those rhetorical sayings that has a ring of truth to it, or perhaps it seemed like that to me in the overwhelmingly heart-breaking context of the film (well, I was only 13). But, in fact, if we love someone and hurt them, deliberately or unintentionally, shouldn't that make us even more willing to apologise?

> I am sorry.
> I was wrong.
> I'll do my best not to do/say this again.
> What can I do to fix this?
> Will you forgive me?

Simple sentences and questions whose language we might vary according to how we naturally express ourselves. Although I'd hope that not every mistake I make warrants all five of them!

And why the tapenade? Because it was at Bar Crystal in Juan les Pins last week, over a glass of rosé wine and their complimentary black olive tapenade, that Tony told me how hurt he'd been by something I'd said. 'I'm sorry' was all I should have said in reply.

Hungry Writing Prompts 36 – 42

Write about behaving badly.

Write about protecting yourself.

Write about a film that made you cry.

Write an apology to someone you love.

Write about your mistakes.

Write about what's easy.

Write about a dish you would serve to say sorry.

BLACK OLIVE TAPENADE

What you need:
- ☐ a large handful of pitted black olives (Crespo's my favourite brand)
- ☐ half a garlic clove
- ☐ two anchovy fillets (or a level teaspoon of *anchoïade*/anchovy paste)
- ☐ chopped coriander or parsley, to taste
- ☐ lemon juice, also to taste
- ☐ about 3 tablespoons of extra virgin olive oil

What you do:
I use a stainless steel vegetable and herb chopper for the olives, garlic, anchovies and herbs in turn, and then mix everything with the oil and lemon juice afterwards but if you have a food processor you could do it all at once. But don't make it into a mush. You want a little bit of texture. A bit like an apology: too smooth and it's just not convincing.

Eat, Laugh, Cry, Remember

Once, on a holiday in Malta, I dressed Tony up in my gypsy skirt and stretchy white vest, used two satsumas for breasts and made up his eyes and lips with the brightest colours I had in my make-up bag. Then I took a photograph. He didn't seem to mind, in fact he seemed quite tickled by the fuss and make-up brushes, but the quantity of rosé we'd shared at Snoopy's restaurant on the seafront in Sliema earlier in the evening might have had something to do with that.

This was 1988. There were no digital cameras for instant viewing (and, praise be, instant deletion). The only instant photographs at the time came courtesy of Polaroid, with their packages of square film and box-like cameras, and slid out of the front of the machine on shiny thick card that everyone huddled over and watched develop. But they tended to be party cameras, appearing at Christmas, birthdays, engagements. You captured your holiday photos on a proper camera, one you had to load and feed film into, then unload and drop off at a chemist's shop to be developed and the prints collected a few days later.

Tony had absolutely no memory of our photo session, or even the haziest recollection of the dressing up that preceded it. His face when I showed him the photo was, appropriately, a picture. Not that he made a particularly good woman – muscled biceps, chest hair and a moustache aren't the most winning of female attributes.

'Nothing?' I said, astonished. 'You can't remember anything?'

'I remember feeling really relaxed. Kind of giggly,' he said. And then, 'You're not going to show anyone that photo, are you?' knowing even as the words left his mouth that his fate was sealed.

Why does this memory push to the front of the queue when I start to write? It's hardly representative of what we've done together during the last 26 years! What about the old barn we renovated? The time we went para-gliding in the Peak District, in the aptly named Hope Valley. Our year in Barcelona. The bookshop we opened. How we coped with illness, death. But no, a tipsy giggle after an evening of garlic mushrooms and grilled chicken is what arrives.

But maybe it's not so surprising. It's a memory full of positive emotion and sensory detail: playfulness, silliness, laughter and touch. And why should there be a hierarchy of memories, my past categorised and filed under importance or triviality with the moments and events I've judged as having changed the direction of my life stacked at the top of the ladder ahead of the time, aged 8, I stared out of my bedroom window into a thunderstorm, worried about my tortoise, Toby, who was out there, somewhere in the garden, alone? So many different things make us who we are.

The Malta memory has one other important ingredient for me too. Food. We went to Snoopy's five times that week. The garlic mushrooms were rich and meaty and topped with melted cheese; the grilled chicken was juicy with a crisp and salty skin. And now I've opened that memory seam, there are more arriving, elbowing one another for room: at the Bar Boya on the stony beach at Cadaques, Spain on my 40th birthday eating fat green olives and slices of the Catalan saucission *fuet*; at Chamonix trying to pierce the braised leg of a *coq* that must have been trekking up and down the Aiguille de Midi for bloody years it was so tough; a filet mignon, 'Pittsburgh', medium rare, served by men in barbershop aprons at Ben Benson's in Manhattan, which put butter to shame for the way it yielded to the edge of a knife.

Over the last quarter of a century food has played a central part in a little ritual we have. At least once a month we sit together in the kitchen, of whatever house we happen to be living in, with French cheese, a good bottle of red opened earlier and left to breathe, crusty bread, olives. We talk and return to each other after travelling separately, physically and emotionally, in other areas of our lives.

In his essay, 'Rather Special and Strangely Popular: A Milk Toast Exemplary'[1] , John Thorne says:

> For an experience to become a ritual … the things involved must be few, so that their meaning is not diffused, and they must somehow assume a perceptible weight. They attain this partly from the reassurance of being "just so", and partly by already possessing the solidity of the absolutely familiar.

Our ritual is not always an occasion of companionship, of reconnection. Sometimes there are difficult things to talk about, resentments and hurts to address. More than once one of us has stormed out, astonished that the other can be so selfish, opinionated, irrational. But 'the solidity of the absolutely familiar' keeps us returning to each other, with the best, and occasionally the worst, twenty six years bring to a table.

We eat, we laugh, we cry. We remember.

---

1 See *Best Food Writing 2010* (De Capo Press Inc., 2010)
http://www.bookdepository.com/book/9780738213811/Best-Food-Writing-2010

Hungry Writing Prompts 43 – 49

Write about a holiday.

Write about forgetting something.

Write about hope.

Write about a thunderstorm.

Write about eating on a beach.

Write about the absolutely familiar.

Write about what hurts you.

Are We All Racists?

I am sitting at the counter of Caviar House & Prunier's Seafood Bar
in Gatwick airport's South Terminal, my ritual pit-stop on flights
between the UK and France.

I've been anticipating this moment ever since I checked in my
luggage, imagining already my plate of Classic Salmon Balik with
sour cream and chopped red onion, the stressful part of the day's
journey over, a sigh as I slip into a contented private space, the ex-
citable buzz in the first sip from a glass of pink champagne.

The Filipino woman behind the bar is preparing lemon slices and
toast.

'He come take your order soon, Madam,' she says smiling at
me, her English a little broken and rushed, and nodding towards a

young man busy with customers at the far end of the bar. Eastern European by the sound of his voice.

'No problem, I'm not in a hurry,' I say and take out my book, a French translation of one of Ian Rankin's Rebus novels, *Fleshmarket Close*. Translated British and American crime novels, or *policiers*, are perfect for improving my French; the narrative tension keeps me turning the pages and the syntax is far less complicated than so much contemporary French literature.

Nous sommes tous racistes, inspecteur…, moi aussi. Ce qui compte, c'est la façon dont nous abordons cette triste réalité. The words of Mohammed Dirwan, a Glasgow lawyer working with immigrants and refugees on the fictional estate of Knoxville. 'We're all racists, inspector…, myself included. What counts is the way we tackle this sad reality.'

I am half-way through my consciousness-changing Balik, and Rebus is contemplating another evening in the company of a bottle of malt, when a female 'cut-glass' English accent to my left grabs my attention.

'You mean *he will come* and take my order,' she says in response to the same greeting I received, her deliberate intonation a lesson in grammar and pronunciation. And not a kind one.

A couple of minutes later she places her order with the young Eastern European man for two spoons of caviar, without a please or thank you, a long manicured nail hovering above her choice on the menu like a treacherous blade. She offers a clipped 'yes' when he suggests a glass of champagne because she's taking so damn long to make up her mind. I might still be staring at the page of my novel, but Rebus and Co have lost my attention.

It doesn't take her long to tip back her head and slip the caviar into her mouth, once, twice, but when the same waiter returns to clear her empty plate and turns away from the bar she impatiently waves him back without a word, at the same time snapping her fingertips at him to indicate she wants to keep the serviette. When he hands her the bill and explains she'll have to pay at another till for the box of Italian biscuits from the wall display she interrupts him sharply. 'I know.' When she leaves she doesn't say thank you or goodbye.

I'm beginning to understand why waiters might spit in someone's food. And I'm also wondering if I'm more irritated than usual by her blatant discourtesy because she's black. When I first turned to look at her the thought spontaneously shot through my mind that one minority group should have more compassion or consideration for another. A 'she should know better' kind of response. An idea that seemed quickly ridiculous in view of racial intolerance, even between people of the same colour, in all parts of the world.

So it's probably her behaviour combined with the Received Pronunciation I associate with privileged and intolerant old colonials that are prickling my Welsh working class sensibilities.

Or maybe, far more straightforwardly, it's the unnecessary rudeness and condescension that I resent. Because the people serving her are friendly and polite and good manners cost nothing. *La politesse, ça ne coûte rien.*

I keep running through the scene during my flight back to Nice, replaying her lines, reviewing my reactions. When I get home I revisit it in conversations with friends. There's no doubt I was initially surprised by her colour after hearing her voice. Is that racist? What counts is how I tackle that reality.

Hungry Writing Prompts 50 – 56

Write about being in an airport.

Write about the first taste of something.

Write about a 'sad reality'.

Write about the voice of someone you cannot see.

Write about a time when you judged someone.

Write about the colour of your skin.

Write about politeness.

Spilt Milk

I have cried over it.

As a kid losing at draughts, dominoes, Monopoly. When I wasn't picked for the three-legged race in my final year at primary school despite winning it for the Green Team for the previous three years. When Maxine McBride chose a new best friend in my first year at comprehensive school. When Mr Warlow, my Welsh teacher, said he was sorry, he'd somehow got things mixed up and I hadn't qualified to recite my hard-learned Welsh poem on the Eisteddfod stage after all. At an 'O' level pass in my 'A' level English Literature. And later, when I was overlooked for a job, a promotion; when I didn't make the competition shortlist, or get the award. When the funding for my first poetry collection was unexpectedly withdrawn. That was a weekend's worth.

We are selling Villa les Marronniers and leaving France. We are part of a statistic that says 50% of Brits who move to France return home within two years, or four in our case by the time we agree the sale. I arrived with plans to speak French fluently, to run creative writing courses on the Côte d'Azur, to live and work here for the next ten years, at least. I am trying not to use the word 'fail'. Because, after all, we have made this house beautiful again, transformed it into a vision of loveliness and light that people stop to

sigh over on Avenue des Chênes. So failure doesn't deserve a place in any deliberations.

Instead, I have decided on, 'It didn't work out'. Perhaps more so for Tony than for me. He has found the language far more of a challenge than he expected, and feels disconnected from the society around him. He has always been far more gregarious than me and misses the ordinary, everyday things he takes for granted in daily life in the UK, from chatting to the woman on the supermarket checkout, to popping along to B&Q on a Sunday morning for some shower sealant, or calling up a friend for an impromptu, last minute drink or dinner.

With hindsight, our decision to deliberately not seek out the expat community when we arrived might have added to his sense of isolation. Not that we've had much time to socialise over the last couple of years as the renovation has been a ten hour a day, seven day a week project that has exhausted us both. But there were other things too: the 'closed shop' system for tradesmen that persists in France means that, as a private individual, he's been unable to access some of the top suppliers of quality building materials; a neighbour's jealous *denoncement* of us to the *Mairie* for repainting the ugly oxblood shutters a beautiful *bleu lavande*, a change which, as we quickly found out, you need official permission for in Antibes. And then there was his accident.

Early one Friday evening at the end of March 2009, just as the light was beginning to drop, he misjudged the height of the blade on the circular saw as he reached over it to steady the piece of wood and sliced almost completely through the fingers and thumb of his left hand, an accident which would leave his hand permanently damaged.

It was only after I left him at the hospital at 10.30 that night, drove home and put away all the tools we'd abandoned in the garden in the rush to get to *Les Urgences*, wiped up the trail of blood over the marble steps to the front door, up the staircase and over the bathroom floor, that I recognised how alone I felt. I'm sure I could have knocked on a neighbour's door; there were one or two people I knew well enough that I could have called. But neither of those things occurred to me at the time. There wasn't anyone I actually wanted or needed to see, no close friends who knew me, who knew us both, friends who would just turn up and let me cry against them.

A few years ago I spoke to a group of anxious writing students about failure. We can't be afraid of failing, because we'll stop growing as writers, I said. We have to look at failure positively. Failure is never about us, it's about development. Failing at something allows us to understand something more about our writing, about ourselves as writers. It means we have the opportunity to take it further.

Positive failure? Yes, why not. We restored a house neglected for 50 years and made it beautiful. For us and for the people who will live here after we have gone. *Elle est belle*. It's beautiful, people say. But *La vie* can be *belle* wherever we are.

Hungry Writing Prompts 57 - 63

Write about something you cried over as a child.

Write about failure.

Write about a conversation between two people in a street.

Write about an accident.

Write about what is beautiful for you.

Write about being alone.

Write about what you miss.

What We Mean When We Say Goodbye

Our final summer in France has been full of hellos and good-byes. Our 17th and 18th staying guests are my youngest step-daughter, Zina, and her son, Oliver, who is seven.

Oliver ate snails for the first time. And olives. And *saucisson*. In fact he ate everything that was put in front of him, the kind of behaviour that astonishes parents who grind their teeth in frustration at home when their kids refuse to eat, or even try, anything new.

'He won't have sauce,' his mother said. 'He never has sauce on anything. No gravy. Nothing.' Ten minutes later he was wolfing down the chicken in a wine and cream sauce his grandad had made.

'If that salami has peppercorns in it…' Yes, but he's already eaten half the packet.

'If you had to give your holiday a score between 1 and 10,' I asked him before he left, 'what would you give it?'

'100,' he said. 'No, 200.'

Sometimes goodbye is hard for the people on both sides of the word

Goodbye: a contraction of 'God be with you.' We want the people we love to be looked after, to stay well, to travel safely. *Adieu*, the French say: 'To God.' And the Spanish too: *Adios*. But what if we don't believe in God, what can we say to people when they leave us?

Pob hwyl, we say in Welsh; *pob* means 'every'. Or we say just *hwyl*, or *hwyl fawr*. *Fawr* means 'big' and *hwyl* can mean 'the sail of a ship' and also 'fun', but it also refers to how people are, their mood. You can sing with *hwyl*, with emotional fervour. And you can ask people how they're feeling: *Sut hwyl sydd arnat ti?* (Literally: 'what kind of feeling, or mood, is on you?')

I like *hwyl fawr* for goodbye. Big feeling. What I want to give away. What I'm grateful to receive.

Hungry Writing Prompts 64 – 70

Write about a summer before things changed.

Write about resistance.

Write about trying something new.

Write about keeping someone safe.

Write about what god is for you.

Write about not getting what you want.

Write about the emotional aspect of saying good-bye.

Open the Box

Food doesn't get prettier than this: steak and potato Cannes style courtesy of the Marriott on *La Croisette*. Okay, the steak does what it says on the menu: chargrilled filet mignon. But the potato. The potato! It said 'salt baked' and I expected a baked potato rubbed with sea-salt, not this jewel: a salt dough crust, its outer skin studded with lavender and rose petals, hugging the potato like a secret.

I like boxes, little containers with lids. They don't have to have any financial value for me to want to keep hold of them once their contents have been used up or kept elsewhere. A plain emerald green box that contained a notebook, a gift from a friend in Hong Kong. A small wooden box that held the gold heart my parents gave me, engraved with the Welsh word, *cariad,* beloved. I still have the jeweller's box my engagement and wedding ring came in, and a porcelain orange that splits in two and was once packed with crystallised orange peel.

The orange is the only one that isn't empty.

It started as a joke, when we first rented an apartment in Juan les Pins while we were house hunting, with a clementine I'd left on my bedside table for three or four days until Tony drew a face on it. Once it was smiling I didn't want to peel it, so I left it to dry out. I can't remember exactly how the second one turned up. I might have mislaid the original and mentioned it to Tony. I might have forgotten about another clementine gathering dust with a pile of books. But now there are two; two leathered and weathered little shrunken heads from a time before we bought *Villa les Marronniers* that have been with me through the challenges and fears and delights of the last four years. Two ugly little suckers that still carry their smiles and a slight scent of Christmas.

I tell myself I am not superstitious, but I won't throw them out. Or I choose not to throw them out for the time being. Perhaps I will when we move back to the UK, perhaps by then I will feel sure that we are back on firm ground, when we're surer of what direction life might take. But now I remember that I wrote a poem about them for Tony, and how could anyone dispose of a muse, however ugly they might be, especially a muse that lives so unassumingly inside a beautiful china orange with a lid?

This is just to say

I still have the two clementines
you drew happy faces on all those years ago
when we were living in the small apartment
with the noisy floors

before we bought the big house
with its big garden, before you hurt your hand,
before we became tired
and felt so far away from home.

They have shrunken and puckered.
Their smiles are crooked.
We can forgive each other the bad times.
Their scent is bitter but rich.

Hungry Writing Prompts 71 – 77

Write about opening a box.

Write about a buying a present.

Write about a joke that's not funny.

Write about loving ugliness.

Write about dust.

Write about your muse.

Write about a bad time.

On Not Remembering

Maybe just saying what it is you can't remember
gets the engine turning over.
        Abigail Thomas, *Thinking About Memoir*

I cannot remember what I had for tea when I came home from
school. Breakfast, yes, dinner between half past twelve and half
past one, yes, but nothing slides onto the plate of my memory for
tea.

I remember the walk home, turning left out of the gates of Tir
Morfa Infants and Juniors, the short stretch of Marine Drive before
turning left again into the top of Chrome Avenue, and how a third
of the way along, where the street curved like the heel of an L, I
used to measure how long it would take before I could make out
our house at the far end.

I remember, after that bend, running with one foot on the kerb,
one foot in the gutter, picking up speed, and the air rushing past me
on the stretch towards home, and misjudging my step on the lip of
the kerb and fracturing my ankle. How Ann, my friend who lived
next door to me, ran ahead to tell my mother while I sat crying, both
feet in the gutter, shocked by how quickly the world could change
and fearful of how long I'd have to stay there, in the middle of the
street where I didn't know anyone.

My world was at 'our end' of the street, small and safe, defined by my family, the kids who lived around us and their parents who were my Uncles and Aunties. Beyond that it was constructed around prescribed routes and stops on different parts of Sandfields Estate. And we never stopped outside the house at the top end of the street where 'The Royal Family' lived, a family the council moved around from street to street, as each house they occupied became uninhabitable: sheets of cardboard stuck against broken window panes, door-frames pulled out and burned for firewood. There was gossip of incest, the father 'interfering with' his daughters, and we'd surreptitiously check out the little kids in the front garden as we passed, looking for what might be proof: a cock-eye, a hair lip, teeth spaced like fence posts.

They were rough, we said. Not like the people at 'our end' of the street. People who went out to work, who paid their rent and bills and kept their gardens looking nice. Though we must have all had our flaws as well, our secrets, things we kept hidden from view: arguments, affairs, breakdowns, drinking. But I still want to say we were not like them. I don't believe we are all the same 'at heart', or 'under the skin', that no one is better than anyone else. Respect has to be better than disrespect. Difference does exist. I'm just not sure where or when it begins.

I remember now. Marie biscuits, Nice biscuits, Jammy Dodgers, Garibaldi, Malted Milk, Custard Creams and, my favourite, Bourbons: chocolate cream sandwiched between two rectangular chocolate biscuits. And sometimes there were sandwiches for tea: cheddar cheese and cucumber, or corned beef, made with thin sliced white bread. 'Squares or triangles?' my mother would ask. Mostly I went for triangles. And sometimes a slice of home-made custard tart made in a deep glass Pyrex dish. My favourite, even when the pastry base had risen up like an arch into the set custard. 'I don't know why that happens sometimes and not others,' my mother used to say.

> …sometimes by stating what you can't remember
> you begin to remember. Make a virtue of the flaw.
> Abigail Thomas, *Thinking About Memoir*

Hungry Writing Prompts 78 - 84

Write about what you can't remember.

Write about the street you lived on as a child.

Write about the journey to or home from school.

Write about a derelict house.

Write about what 'difference' means to you.

Write about virtues and flaws.

Write about what you remember.

Take One Red Dragon

Every year on 1st March – St David's Day, *Dydd Dewi Sant*, dedicated to the patron saint of Wales – I wore my Welsh national costume to primary school: a black felt hat, a small white apron over my kilt, and, pinned to my plaid shawl, a fresh daffodil from the garden whose big trumpet head bumped my chin, releasing the sprinkle and scent of pollen. The boys wore leeks attached to their jumpers with nappy-sized safety pins, until playtime, when some show-off would decide to eat his raw.

There was a school concert, and we sang Welsh hymns and folk songs: *Calon Lân* (Pure Heart) and *Oes gafr eto,* a song about white, blue and red goats which had to be sung faster and faster with each successive verse until the words fell apart in our mouths. The finale of the concert was usually a play in Welsh written by one of the teachers.

When I was ten I was picked for the leading role of Maggi, an enterprising cook named for a 1960s' packet soup, who, in the days before political correctness, convinced a bunch of hungry and half-naked schoolboy cannibals not to boil the poor missionary, complete with pith helmet, but to add a packet of her tasty powdered soup to their cardboard cauldron instead. *Flasus iawn!* Very tasty! It was one of the more enjoyable moments of my early associations with non-conformist religion.

I only recently discovered that my Welsh costume was not 'traditional' at all, but a 19th century invention by Lady Llanover, a Welsh heiress and patron of the arts, born near Abergavenny in South Wales. She took certain items from the clothing of Welsh countrywomen at the time, added some Welsh tweed, and created a national dress that would take hold of the public imagination and survive until today. To be fair, Lady Llanover was not the only one tinkering with the recipe for welsh identity. During the 18th and 19th centuries other popular symbols of Wales – the red dragon, leeks, harps and druids, and even some bardic rituals – were also introduced, part of a pressing cultural wave to identify and strengthen the idea of welshness in response to social changes that were threatening traditional ways of life.

Change can often be a catalyst for us to protect what we deem to be under threat. Perhaps it is partly because I have lived away from Wales for more than thirty five years that I cling to the small yearly ritual of making Welshcakes on St David's Day, wherever I am and for whoever I'm around: friends, family, writing groups, my university students, and neighbours. And even though they could be a result of a similar mythmaking, not particularly Welsh at all but common to an early baking practice of cooking on stone in front of an open fire, I still associate them with growing up in Wales and they form part of my perception of what it means, or feels like, to be Welsh.

But a Welshcake isn't really a cake. And neither is it a scone, or a biscuit. 'Oh, they're drop-scones,' some people say when I describe how they're cooked on a griddle, or a bakestone, a *maen* or a *planc* (depending on which part of Wales you are from). But they're not that either. For a start, they're made from soft dough not a batter, dough that plumps on a hot griddle with the scent of nutmeg and butter. They are my mother's cool hands, perfect for baking. They are home.

Hungry Writing Prompts 85 – 91

Write about dressing up.

Write about singing.

Write about boys at school.

Write about something you believed to be true
but later turned out to be false.

Write about food that reminds you of home.

Write about plumpness.

Write about your mother's hands.

WELSHCAKES

Depending on which part of Wales you're in you might hear them called *Tishan ar y ma'n* (teeshun arr uh maan) or *Pice ar y Maen* (peekay arr uh mine).

What you need:
- ☐ ½ lb self-raising flour
- ☐ pinch of salt
- ☐ ¼ level teaspoon of ground nutmeg
- ☐ 4 oz butter, left to soften slightly at room temperature
- ☐ 4 oz sugar
- ☐ 2 oz seedless raisins or sultanas
- ☐ 1 egg, beaten
- ☐ milk to mix
- ☐ caster sugar to sprinkle

What you do:
- ☐ Sift flour, spice and salt into a large bowl and rub in the butter with your fingertips until the mixture resembles fine breadcrumbs. (That's what my school cookery teacher always said!)
- ☐ Mix in the sugar and fruit
- ☐ Make a well in the middle of the bowl and add the beaten egg
- ☐ Working in a circle, push the dry mixture into the liquid centre with your hand, until it binds to a soft dough adding some milk if necessary
- ☐ Roll out the dough on a floured surface to a thickness of about ¼ inch and use a pastry cutter to make rounds. The size is up to you, but my favourite is a dinky 1½ inch fluted cutter which makes between 25 and 30 little welshcakes
- ☐ Cook them in small batches on a pre-heated non-stick griddle, or a large heavy-bottomed frying pan, over a low to medium heat, for about 2 minutes each side, or until golden brown
- ☐ Sprinkle well with caster sugar while still warm

I think they're at their best at this point, but if you microwave a cold one for 10 seconds you'll recover some of that original airiness. Or, try spreading one with soft, unsalted butter. Or a dollop of crème fraiche. Or both.

Figs and Doors Opening

Yesterday evening we said goodbye to the last of our summer guests. The last guest we'll ever have here. Today I'm packing and closing up the house as we leave tomorrow morning

for two weeks in the UK. Then we'll be back for a month to finalise the sale and move permanently back to Kent.

I'm putting aside the fridge goods, fruit and snacks we'll take with us for the journey, and calculating how much Tony and I can manage to eat of what's left. I think watermelon does go with chopped cold chicken in crème fraiche, mayonnaise and curry spices. Well, it will today. There's also a lonely *Mille Feuille* in the fridge and I'll bet money Tony will get to that before I do!

Some of what's left is breaking my heart. Figs. Our three fig trees are plump with fruit that's now ripening on a daily basis. I'll take a bowl of them with us in the car and I've told my house and cat-sitter to pick and eat as many as she wants. And I'm hoping there'll be a few unctuous ones left when we get back at the end of the month so I can make fig tart or jam.

We don't stop for proper meals during the 650 mile drive. Instead we have brief grazing sessions in a few of the bountiful, and often very beautiful, French *aires*: rest-stops with picnic tables, trees and toilets, that are dotted along the *autoroutes* that lead us west then

north towards Calais. They put British motorways and service stations to shame.

We picnic on hard-boiled eggs with celery salt, fresh tomatoes, peppered salami, some creamy French cheese, a baguette, scooped up at a petrol station that always fills the back of the car with the scent of its fresh-baked crust. Even the thought of this today comforts me a little when I think about the 12 hours on the road.

And the figs, of course. These little green baubles heavy with sweet pink flesh. They will always remind me of our house in Antibes, wherever I am in the future. How the sunlight slices through the lavender shutters. The red tiled staircase that curls and rises through four storeys. The smell of the sea that arrives in our garden on the breeze rolling up Avenue des Chênes.

There's a line from a poem of mine that we painted on the paving stones in the garden between the Plane trees that guard the marble steps to the front door. I wonder if the new owners will keep it?

> *une lumiere qui me fait penser à des clefs de porte et je*
> *suis la porte qui s'ouvre*
> a light that makes me think of keys to a door and
> I am the door opening

I always want to be the door that opens.

Hungry Writing Prompts 92 – 98

Write about the last person to leave.

Write about packing a suitcase.

Write about what's left over.

Write about picking fruit from a tree.

Write about a picnic.

Write about climbing the stairs.

Write about a door opening.

Goodwill, Happy Companionship and Saying Thank-you to the Chicken

meant to take a photo of the roast chicken and roast vegetables we had for dinner last night, but it was only when our plates were a smear of *jus* and breadcrumbs that I remembered.

We've been a little tense since when we arrived back in the south of France last week, partly due to the wilting humidity and partly due to the last minute demands of our buyer's English solicitor who seems to want official *attestations* for even the air we breathe!

But mealtimes are the moments we look forward to.

> Eating is not merely a material pleasure. Eating well gives a spectacular joy to life and contributes immensely to goodwill and happy companion-ship. It is of great importance to the morale.
>
> Elsa Schiaparelli[2]

Robin Fox, the anthropologist, talks about the ceremony attached to eating and how the contemporary ease of obtaining food, and the

---

2 BrainyQuote.com. Retrieved 7 July 2015, http://www.brainyquote.com/quotes/quotes/e/elsaschiap142633.html

advent of fast food in particular, has resulted in it losing its significance for us:

> "It's like the American Indians. When they killed a deer, they said a prayer over it," says Fox. "That is civilization. It is an act of politeness over food. Fast food has killed this. We have reduced eating to sitting alone and shoveling it in. There is no ceremony in it."[3]

Ceremony. Unfortunately, the word's root in the Latin *caerimonia* (religious worship) doesn't do it any favours. It evokes a formality and solemnity I don't associate with the joy of eating with family and friends.

Tony tells the story of attending a Showmen's Guild Ball at Grovesnor House in London when he was 18. He was dating the then President's daughter, and was completely unprepared for the formality of the evening: the Master of Ceremonies, the endless courses and the array of required cutlery fanning out to his right and left across the white linen tablecloth. Not being the kind of person to admit defeat he decided to pick up and use whatever seemed appropriate as each course arrived, and felt he was doing quite well until dessert was served and he had to ate his Peach Melba with a soup spoon and a fish knife.

So if it's not ceremony that I want and need in shared meals, what is it?

My great-nephew, Iwan, who is three and a half, recently made a return visit to a family holiday flat in Freshwater East, West Wales.

'Flat, I have missed you,' he said to the air and walls when he walked in.

I think that's the kind of simple and honest ceremony I want to have at meals.

Chicken, you were delicious, so crispy-skinned and tender-fleshed. Thank you.

---

3   From 'The Magic of the Family Meal', Nancy Gibbs, *Time Magazine*, June 4th 2006

Hungry Writing Prompts 99 – 105

Write about forgetting.

Write about a moment of tension.

Write about happy companionship.

Write about a first date.

Write about a formal event or occasion.

Write about air.

Write about saying, 'Thank you'.

Cruelty and Kindness

once made the girl who lived next door to me drink mud. The fact I was only 5 or 6, and this was a pretend tea-party where we'd mixed up earth and water to resemble hot chocolate in the blue plastic teacups, might go some way towards mitigating my behaviour, but the memory remains harsh.

There were three of us at the tea-party: the little girl next door, me and my best friend and it was, perhaps, that intimacy between the two of us that engendered a streak of cruelty towards the 'outsider'.

'You have to drink it if you want to play with us.' I remember us pressurising her.

And she did. Or at least I remember watching the mud seep between her closed lips. And I think she might have cried.

Cruelty could be too strong a word here; bullying may be more appropriate although that doesn't make the memory any less unpleasant. Some people might interpret the whole event as part of any child's introduction to social dynamics, the emotional experiences of inclusion and exclusion. Others might say that what adults perceive as cruelty in very young children is often only curiosity: a desire to know the result of a particular action. And perhaps I'm making too much of it, searching too deeply for a meaning that might not be there.

I think I remember feeling guilty later that day, or at least uneasy about the way I acted. I hope I did. I hope it was an early lesson in self-reflection and it affected how I treated people from that time on.

Hungry Writing Prompts 106 – 112

Write about a memory that makes you feel uncomfortable.

Write about applying pressure.

Write about exclusion.

Write about being curious.

Write about the girl next door.

Write about a lesson learned.

Write about kindness.

Dreams and Transformations

The bird in my dream is tame. It sits on my hand while I am standing outside my house in Kent. It bathes in water I pour into a hollow in the tarmac right next to my feet. When it presses against my leg it changes into a grey floppy-eared puppy with a thick suede collar around its neck printed with a message: *This dog is looking for a home. If it is returned to the address noted it will be destroyed.*

Dreams are full of transformations. We walk into one house and find ourselves in a different place entirely. We talk to people we know who don't look like the people we know. When we dream we're supposed to be always dreaming about ourselves, each symbol representing some aspect of our character, our psyche.

Between the age of 8 and 9, in my second year at junior school, I had recurring nightmares about mushrooms and telegraph poles. The mushroom nightmares were more a feeling rather than dreams of real mushrooms but 'mushroom' was the only way I could describe them at the time. Imagine yourself about to tip over into sleep then, at the edge of your perception, something soft and silent begins to expand, pushing against you, filling the space until there is no room for you, until you're on the verge of disappearing. You cannot breathe.

The telegraph poles nightmare was more straightforward. I am passing them or perhaps they are passing me, but I am counting them. But they get faster and faster until I can't keep up. My head spins. I feel sick and wake up crying.

My first year in Junior School had been in Mrs Bamford's class. I remember making salt dough jam tarts. I remember her telling us about Winston Churchill's death; the photo of a fat man with a cigar that she showed us in the newspaper. Mrs Bamford had Mary Poppins hair.

Mr Davies was my teacher the following year. He was a thin, worn out looking man who wore a suit the colour of tobacco and a hand-knitted waistcoat. He disapproved of us playing with the Plasticine. If we made mistakes in our exercise books he hurled them from his desk across the room at us. We were 8 and 9. Once, when I was tucking a doll into her pram he told me it didn't matter how many blankets I added because it wouldn't make her any warmer. I remember feeling upset, but angry too, angry because, in the way children do, I suspected there was truth in what he was saying and I didn't want it to be true.

The Times Tables were the focus of Mr Davies's class, which we had to memorie and recite. Like most kids, I found 1 to 6 not too bad, but the trouble started with 7, 8 and then 9.

> One 9 is 9
> Two 9s are 18
> Three 9s are 27
> Four 9s are 36
> Five 9s are 45
> Six 9s are…

Even today, when I recite it out loud, I can feel the flutter of small panic in my chest as I pass, *Five 9s are 45…*

After months of being woken almost every night by my screams my parents went to the school and complained about Mr Davies's behaviour in the classroom. My mother remembers the headmaster saying, 'He suffers with his nerves.' But whatever the headmaster said or did must have worked. Mr Davies's demeanour changed overnight, and my nightmares stopped shortly afterwards.

The dream I recalled at the beginning makes sense on some levels. I have left France and moved back to our house in Kent. If I am both the bird and the dog then I have relinquished the air for the earth, flight for firm ground. An old home for a new home. Perhaps I never lived long enough in France to feel 'earthed'. Or perhaps the dream means nothing at all: a garbled collage of random images I am trying to make sense of. Because that's what we try to do: make sense of things in the life we live, the real and the imagined. Although when I walk through the apple orchards around our house, through the long grass, look up at the skyline fired by sunset, it all makes perfect sense.

So much of what we believe, or what we feel, perhaps even of who we think we are, seems to be dependent on the moment we are living in, the world we experience in the precise and elusive present.

Hungry Writing Prompts 113 – 119

Write about something that changes over time: a person, a relationship, a journey.

Write about dreaming.

Write about a teacher you had at school.

Write about not wanting something to be true.

Write about flight.

Write about firm ground.

Write about what you are experiencing right now, in this moment.

The Cooked and the Cruel

Where does the love of food end and cruelty begin? I'm sure there will be different boundaries among us, and contradictions too. I'll start with myself: I will only buy free range eggs but I ate *foie gras* many times during my four years in France. I refuse to buy the battery chickens from the supermarket but I don't question the source of the pork in Tesco Finest Cumberland Sausages. Actually, that sounds more like hypocrisy than contradiction.

I am reading *Breakfast with Socrates* by Robert Rowland Smith, a series of philosophical commentaries on the ordinary content of our day to day lives, from getting ready to go out, sitting at a desk, going to a party, to falling asleep at the end of the day. In the chapter, 'Cooking and Eating Dinner', he describes the French penchant for ortolan, a 'delicacy' I'd never heard of that has been illegal in France since 1999, although the laws have only been properly enforced since 2007. I should warn you that it doesn't make for easy reading:

> The ortolan – a bunting, the size of a sparrow – is trapped and incarcerated in a windowless box to be fed figs; when it has fattened, it is literally drowned in Armagnac, its minute lungs flooded with the rasping liquor. Now dead, it is

plucked, roasted and served whole – bones, guts, pluck and all – with only the head to be left dangling untouched beyond the eater's lips.

François Mitterrand, the former French president, allegedly ate ortolan at his 'last supper' while terminally ill with prostate cancer, with his head concealed beneath the traditional napkin. The reasons for the napkin are disputed: it's a messy business crunching through bones and innards; it preserves the aromas; it hides your face from God. Mitterand died eight days later.

Of course I prefer to think that my unquestioning purchase of pork sausages is on a different level to Mitterand's ortolan feast. And perhaps, to some degree, it is if I believe the supermarket's claims about animal welfare.

But the ortolan story has been playing on my mind since I read it.

> … just as either the over ripeness [pheasant, cheese] or the rawness [sushi, steak tartare] of what you serve can speak to your cultivation, to your acquired level of artistry, so cruelty can exhibit your refinement.

So what will I do the next time I'm in a restaurant and really fancy the *foie gras*? Ask if it comes from a duck or goose that hasn't been subjected to *gavage* or force-feeding? Some top chefs, including Anthony Bourdain, have supported foie gras production from humanely treated, properly raised ducks so, in theory, it should be available. But could I be sure?

The last time I checked there was a Michelin-starred restaurant in 'idyllic Berkshire', England, called L'Ortolan, although the little bird on their logo looks quite happy, and I'm delighted to report there's no trace of the barbaric dish on any of their menus. But still, I'm sure I can hear a mournful tweet between the syllables every time I say the name out loud.

Hungry Writing Prompts 120 – 126

Write about one item of food you couldn't do without.

Write about cruelty.

Write about 'a last supper'.

Write about watching someone eat.

Write about bones.

Write about what you're unsure of.

Write about something you don't like in yourself.

Now

Not long before they all come home, before they re-fill the house with chatter and laughter. Not long before the cork pops from a chilled bottle of wine, a beer is opened, toys spill across the wooden floor. Before the chicken is pulled from the oven and set to rest, before the potatoes are tipped into sizzling oil. But for now the house is quiet; the kids' bright paintings on the kitchen wall, the oven light and the fluffed up flesh of par-boiled potatoes the only hints of what soon will be.

I am at my niece's house, while she's out for the day, preparing a late Sunday lunch for our extended family. I've hit the slow time: all the vegetables prepared and par-cooked, the chicken on its last half-hour, the gravy and stuffing made. The house feels so quiet I notice my own breathing.

I used to fill silence. For years, when I was alone, I'd put the television or radio on for company, a request for activity and sound to distract me, to prevent me from looking inwards and not liking the silence I found there: silence that felt closer to emptiness than peace. I think that started to change when I began writing at the age of 30 and felt fulfilled in a way I never had before. It sounds simplistic, and perhaps a little melodramatic, but I remember it as my first real passion: something that was a part of me but which existed separately from me as well, something that was a bridge between me and the exterior world, a world that now seemed ripe with opportunities and possibilities. I wonder sometimes about writers who say they have always written, who were assembling home-made books as children and cobbling together novels during their teens. Did that sense of belonging to something, of something belonging to them, at such a young age, make life seem less intimidating, more negotiable? Or did those gifts bring their own insecurities? And I wonder too if some kind of self-fulfilment, a commitment to an idea, or a practice that transcends the limited visions we have of ourselves, is something we all need to feel truly contented?

The back door opens. My sister comes in with a bottle of champagne. Her cheek is cool when I kiss it. Her husband shakes out the Sunday paper. With the slam of a car-door on the drive, my niece and her husband are back with two flushed and excited kids. And all that matters is now, this moment, how they press themselves against me smelling of ice-cream and grass and afternoon sun.

Hungry Writing Prompts 127 - 133

Write about an empty house.

Write about a child's drawing.

Write about breathing.

Write about filling the silence.

Write about belonging to someone or something.

Write about sisters.

Write about the smell of grass.

MY BEST ROAST POTATOES

It was an American friend, back in 1988, who told me about using dried oregano for roast potatoes and I've added it ever since.

What you need:
- ☐ King Edward or Maris Piper potatoes
- ☐ olive oil
- ☐ dried oregano
- ☐ dried minced garlic (it has to be dried as fresh will burn and taste bad)

What you do:
- ☐ Peel and half, or quarter, your potatoes, depending on the size
- ☐ Rinse well to get rid of the starch and bring to the boil in salted water
- ☐ Simmer over a medium heat for between 3 or 4 minutes. As someone who has ended up with mashed potatoes for lunch, instead of the planned roast, I know how important it is to time this. The tip of a sharp knife should just be able to pierce the flesh
- ☐ Drain well. No, drain them *really* well
- ☐ Tip them back into the dry saucepan, put on the lid and give them a little bang about to fluff up the outsides then leave them uncovered in the saucepan or a dish. You can do all this in advance, and it's what gives you a lovely crispiness
- ☐ Heat 4 to 6 tablespoons of olive oil in a roasting pan in the top of a hot oven for about 4 minutes. You want it to be hot enough to sizzle when you tip in the potatoes
- ☐ And tip
- ☐ And stir them around and make sure they're all covered with the oil
- ☐ Sprinkle on the oregano and garlic and cook for around 45 minutes until lovely and golden and speckly
- ☐ You can flip them all over half way through if you like, but if you made sure they were all covered in oil at the beginning you shouldn't need to

The Invention of the Crisp Sandwich

The first crisps of my childhood were Smith's. They were plain in a way that kids today could not conceive of: potato, nothing else. But there was the excitement of rifling through the contents for the little twist of blue paper containing salt so you could season to your own preference. The 'twist' became a sachet, and then that disappeared too with the introduction of ready-flavoured crisps.

Smoky Bacon, Roast Chicken, Cheese & Onion, Prawn Cocktail —I tried them for their novelty factor, but the flavours never seemed to live up to the promise written on the packet.

Salt & Vinegar crisps were the star of one particular December afternoon just before Christmas in the mid-1960s. These were the days of milkmen, bread vans, door to door rent collections and insurance men calling round to pick up premiums and my mother always had the weekly payments ready, counted out into little plastic bags tucked into the kitchen drawer next to the oven.

Aunty Beryl-next-door had already alerted her to the imminent arrival of the insurance man who'd been toasting Christmas at a number of houses as he made his way down the street. By the time he reached us at number 73 he was, to be 1960s polite, rather the worse for wear, but to use a contemporary vernacular, completely off his face.

Drunkenness wasn't a state I was familiar with. I vaguely understood how 'tipsy' or 'one pint too many' revealed itself in adults on New Year's Eve but he had attained a state of jollification I had never before witnessed. And he was giving away money, literally throwing it across the living room: big pre-decimalisation bronze pennies stamped with the head of Britannia. But as quickly as I collected them in my hot little hands my mother insisted that I gave them back.

These were also the days before drinking and driving restrictions, and offering a little Christmas drink and a few crisps was usual behaviour, but my mother also did her best to ply him with as much black coffee as he'd drink.

'Let me make you a sandwich too,' she offered.

And he accepted the bread and butter, but insisted on introducing us to the crisp sandwich.

My sandwiches had always come in single varieties from a predetermined list: cheese, corned beef, cucumber, or tinned salmon. They were soft and flat. But here were sandwiches breaking the rules, noisy sandwiches, their filling crushed flat in his big hands, splintering around the edges of the bread as he took a bite. I joined in, enthusiastically.

I couldn't wait for him to call again the following week, the funny man who made crisp sandwiches, threw pennies around the room and made me laugh.

'Do you remember what you did last time?' I said cheerfully, when he came into the kitchen. And I wilted under the weight of my mother's glare, his sheepish downward glance, and the raw realisation of having said something I shouldn't have. The fun was over.

And, I think, so was his job. As far as I can remember we never saw him again and someone else took over his round. I wonder if he's still alive, if he remembers that afternoon? If he does, is it with regret, embarrassment or indifference? Would it mean anything to him that his story remains with me, nearly 50 years later? That I smile, fondly, every time I remember him?

Hungry Writing Prompts 134 – 140

Write about something that disappeared.

Write about a man who came to your house.

Write about making a sandwich.

Write about drunkenness.

Write about throwing something across a room.

Write about being ashamed.

Write about someone's smile.

The Second Bottle of Wine Argument

You've shared and enjoyed a good bottle of wine, and you don't really need any more to drink, but hey … you're feeling good, relaxed, you could sit here all night chatting, so why not order or open another?

It's usually half way through the second bottle that the accumulative effect of alcohol makes one of you brave, rash or stupid enough to bring up a subject that would be better discussed in a more sober condition. There's a straightening of spine, a narrowing of eyes … if you listened carefully you'd probably hear knives sharpening themselves close by. But you're both blind and deaf to the signs of danger and you charge ahead.

Of course, the second bottle of wine isn't always guaranteed to invoke an argument, but I have met a lot of couples who identify with it. My own most volatile experience of the phenomenon, which was compounded by a particularly dodgy moussaka (bad food always makes me grumpy), took place at an open-air restaurant in Heraklion, Crete and peaked when Tony said, 'That's not an opinion!' and I stood up, hurled the napkin holder across the table at him, and stormed off into the dark streets hoping I could remember where the hotel was. I did.

And, breathe…

I suppose all that's necessary is a moment of reflection as one of you pops the second cork. You could remind yourselves, silently, to keep the conversation light and avoid the following topics:

- ☐ criticising the other one's children
- ☐ any comments or suggestions that the other one's family members might be irresponsible, selfish or immature
- ☐ any self-improvement tips
- ☐ starting a sentence with 'It's probably not the best time to say this but...'
- ☐ telling a woman not to get emotional
- ☐ telling a man, 'Look who's getting emotional now'

But in my experience true clarity is a rare thing at the end of a first bottle, and it seems that once you enter 'the valley of death' there's nothing you can do except to keep on riding until one of you falls off your horse.

Hungry Writing Prompts 141 - 147

Write about a time you said something then wished you could take it back.

Write about blindness.

Write about the signs of danger.

Write about a dark street.

Write about someone else's children.

Write about a rare thing.

Write about falling.

More

the heart of a bonsai grove

Two old ladies in the Japanese Garden remind me of exotic finches in their turquoise and black pants suits, lips painted red, white hair coiffeured and lacquered: their tiny bones weighed down with too many bright feathers. They cling to each other as they totter on each step towards the Museum's doors, then pause at the top to look behind them, at the lake with its reflections of sky and trees. If I clapped my hands suddenly, they might take flight, across the water, rising over the umbrella pines and bamboo grove, their wings stretching in the warm air as if they'd never feared falling, never doubted that earthbound was just a passing phase.

There is always more to know about the world: like this Japanese Garden in South Florida. Always more to know about myself: like how I can feel simultaneously ecstatic and uncomfortable. Sitting alone in the restaurant, overlooking the lake at the Morikami Museum & Gardens there's the joy of being exactly where I want to be and choosing whatever I want to eat and in whatever order I want to eat it. There's no-one to express astonish-

ment or disagree, or suggest something else. If I want to start with dessert I can. But every other table in the café is lively with chatter and chopsticks, which seems to exaggerate the silence and emptiness at mine. I have left the museum guide open on the table next to my napkin, a notebook and a pen beside it, and while I'd like to put them away, to be uncluttered, I'd feel too exposed if I did. They fill some of the space around me, like laying down a blanket on the grass in a park, defining my boundaries, creating a small known world for me to occupy.

I order chilled tofu with soy-garlic sauce, finely sliced spring onions and pink leaves of pickled ginger, Chef Fu's crab cakes and bang-bang shrimp, and a bowl of edamame beans.

I'm in Japanese gastronomy heaven, swaying deliciously between silken and crunchy, sweet and sour, cool and spicy. I try a steamed edamame bean, which looks so much like a sugar-snap pea that I pop the whole thing into my mouth and immediately wish there was someone sitting opposite me. Someone who will laugh with me while I choke and spit out a masticated lump of woody pod. Perhaps the waiter turning over the bowl's deep lid and leaving it on the table was a clue, but I'm still not absolutely sure of edamame protocol and I can't see anyone else eating them to pick up some tips. Maybe I was unlucky with a particularly woody pod, but they all seem equally tough between my fingers and bristly too, like the skin of a little pig. So I decide to pop the pods and trickle the beans onto my plate.

While I didn't laugh at loud I did smile and chuckle quietly to myself. Though it wasn't so long ago when a similar gaffe would have had me squirming with embarrassment. Perhaps age has helped me take myself less seriously, made it easier to laugh at myself. Or perhaps I've made myself look ridiculous so many times now that I've begun to enjoy it.

During an Adult Education writing workshop a number of years ago I invited the group to contribute a verb, a noun, an emotion, a time, and an adjective for a 10 minute spontaneous writing exercise … *dreaming, a house, regret, late afternoon and … fluffy*. Fluffy? Seriously? But spontaneous means running with whatever's suggested so we all began to write.

I like this kind of exercise, how people create different worlds from the exactly the same material so it's great when students are happy to share their free-writing afterwards.

'I'm afraid I haven't used "house",' one student apologised before she read. 'But I do have my character looking out of a bedroom window.'

'That's fine,' I said. 'You have an implied house.' And, in a rather more enthusiastic manner than I intended, 'I have an implied fluffy.'

Really?!

Hungry Writing Prompts 148 – 154

Write about old women.

Write about reflections in water.

Write about visiting a museum.

Write about doing whatever you want to do.

Write about a blanket on the grass.

Write about getting older.

Write about regret.

James Bond, Licence to Cook

saw the movie *Goldfinger* at Butlins holiday camp at Pwllheli in North Wales in the summer of 1966. A woman painted gold. Quite a lot of kissing. And a man called Oddjob who sliced off people's heads with his bowler hat. My sister and I blinked out of the cinema into the heat and light of an afternoon we'd forgotten was there. At eight and eleven it was the first 'grown-up' film we'd seen, and it was even more special to us because a Welsh woman, Shirley Bassey, belted out the title song that was still ringing in our ears.

I watched it again on TV last week. This time around different things made an impression:

- the champagne: Dom Perignon '53
- the meltingly good cut of Connery's clothes (the all-in-one towelling sun-suit aside)
- the not-so-good join in his toupée
- the women's pointy triangular breasts
- the theme: the obliteration of the world economy, which these days doesn't even have a glimmer of fantasy about it.

About ten years ago we stayed in a little villa on Hillsboro Beach, north of Fort Lauderdale on Florida's Atlantic coast over Christmas and New Year. Spike TV were running back to back Bond movies, so on Christmas Day, while I alternately sipped champagne, roasted chicken and potatoes, read in the sun for stretches of 30 minutes, and thickened the gravy with pancake mix because I'd forgotten to buy flour, Tony leaned back into the villa's 'massage' leather arm chair, complete with remote control and adjustable foot and head-rests, dressed in a sarong, with a glass of Buck's Fizz in his hand.

'Where's my woman?' he hollered playfully when the commercials came on.

The name's Crosse, Tony Crosse.

We always had turkey for Christmas when I was little. We woke up to one of Dad's big socks at the end of the bed, plump with rolled-up comics and a Satsuma tucked into the toe. Mammy put a three-penny bit in the home-made Christmas pudding. There were Selection Boxes, a tin of Quality Street, After Eights, mince pies. Dad drank beer. Mammy drank Harvey's Bristol Cream, and our sips progressed over the years to a half of a very small sherry glass with dinner. And we listened to the Queen at 3 o'clock. The five of us together.

There's something very satisfying about shared and repeated occasions, those moments or events when we feel connected to people or place. When we feel we belong. They don't have to be rituals dictated by religion or society. They don't have to contain any overt sense of ceremony. All they need is conscious thought to give them significance and a mood of celebration.

When my great-nephew, Iwan, hears that I'm coming to Wales his response is generally, 'Straws and crisps?' I am that woman! Our impromptu parties with balloons and games (and 'straws and crisps') bind us.

Connery's early Bond movies have now become a Christmas ritual. The holiday's just not the same without James.

Hungry Writing Prompts 155 – 161

Write about going to the cinema.

Write about the first sip of champagne.

Write about a childhood Christmas.

Write about an adult Christmas.

Write about something a child told you.

Write about a ritual, something you repeat during the year or from year to year.

Write about James Bond.

Desperate for a McDonald's

A few years ago the local news in South Wales covered a story about a man who crashed his car into McDonald's because they refused to serve him in the drive-thru hatch: he was on foot.

I know what you're thinking: why didn't he take his car into the drive-thru in the first place? The eight pints of lager probably had something to do with it. Maybe he thought he was in his car.

When the staff told him to go into the restaurant he went to get his (real) car, parked it on the kerb and walked back (I guess you can't fix stupid) to the drive-thru hatch again, and continued making a fuss at which point they refused to serve him anywhere.

'You'd better move yourself, I am coming in. Even if I've got to ram these doors down, I am coming in.' That's the voice of a man desperate for a McDonald's.

In true tabloid style the manager was quoted as describing the situation as 'carnage'. No, carnage is the destruction of the rain forest. Carnage is factory farming. And maybe it's killing people slowly with sugar too. But where does corporate responsibility end and personal responsibility begin? No one's force feeding us burgers and nuggets. We are doing it to ourselves.

Tony says that when he sees the big bar of Galaxy chocolate on the coffee table he can feel his jaws starting to ache for it, his mouth begin to salivate. 'I could easily eat the whole thing,' he says. 'I have to stop myself.'

When I watch McDonald's TV advert for their breakfast wrap – sausage, bacon, egg, potato rosti and cheese lovingly folded into a wheat wrap – I want one. I really want one. (I'm developing a slim vein of empathy for the South Wales drunk.) What can be wrong with it?

According to McDonald's website they use free range eggs and pork sourced from British farms. They have a sustainable seafood strategy and recycle their cooking oil. They campaign against litter and use low energy lamps in their restaurants. They employ 80,000 people in the UK and run an education programme. In the last 20 years they've built 14 Ronald McDonald Houses to provide accommodation for families with children in hospital. The Sunday Times says they're the best big company to work for. McDonald's are starting to sound like the Mother Theresa of the corporate world. Crikey, they've even received three awards from the RSPCA.

It's often easier to accept pre-packaged arguments from both defenders and attackers of any issue rather than sift through vast amounts of information to find our own truth. But for now I'm sticking with my personal boycott of McDonald's at least until they start using free range chicken meat and stop barrelling sugar into their bread and fries.

I realise some people might think me overly critical and pedantic. Even Michael Pollan, at the end of his book *Food Rules, An Eater's Manual*, quotes Oscar Wilde's 'All things in moderation. Including moderation.' And says, 'Break the Rules once in a while'. And yes, I can go along with that. But I'm even more inclined to agree with his Rule 20: 'It's not food if it arrived through the window of your car.'

Hungry Writing Prompts 162 – 168

Write about desperation.

Write about refusing to do what you're told.

Write about what kills us.

Write about the longing for something.

Write about take-away food.

Write about what's right in the world.

Write positively about someone or something you doubt.

Trouble

learnt the secret of a good Bolognese sauce from a man who looked like George Best.

It was 1979. I met him at the bar of Lord's Discotheque on Jersey in the Channel Islands where I was working, transferred there

by the Midland Bank in South Wales the year before. His name was Joe. He drove tourist coaches for a living, he said, and came from Argentina.

I don't know if he was a particularly good liar, or perhaps a particularly good impersonator – he even went to the trouble of carrying a coach driver's licence tag on his key-ring – but I was twenty-one and particularly naïve. I believed that his jealousy, sullen moods and tendency to show up at my place at all times of the day and night were proof that he loved me.

This was my first ever Bolognese, courtesy of Robert Carrier, whose precise instructions I followed to the letter, slice and ounce for hours on a Sunday morning. Joe was due at my flat at one o'clock. He turned up two hours later in full defensive bluster, blaming a football game he'd forgotten about, trying to make me laugh about the whole thing, and, when that failed, resorting to loud threats of leaving. He didn't have to stay and put up with this kind of shit. He'd had a tough enough week at work without his girlfriend giving him a hard time at the weekend. He was going to walk out and not come back. Go on then, I say from 35 years away, walk out and keep on walking, you arrogant prick.

And I want to shake her, that girl who starts crying. 'Don't go. I'm sorry. Please stay,' she says because she's frightened, because she feels she's in the wrong, because she can't see she has a choice.

I can come up with any number of excuses for my reaction, then and on later occasions. I didn't have any strong, independent, female role models. I had no self-belief. I used to mistake a man shouting for authority. I can cite my family background, the social era in South Wales where I grew up, the bank I worked for, which had different ideas about work, approval and promotion for men and women. They all sound self-pitying.

How long did I carry on seeing him? Six months, nine months? Until after I found out he was married and ran a hotel with his wife. Until after he was taken into police custody one Friday night, accused of stealing drums of coffee and fillet steaks from a Cash & Carry, and coerced me into being his alibi. Until after his wife phoned me at work one day and said, 'You think you're special? You're just one in a long line of girls. He always comes back to me, you'll see.'

She was right.

Joe wasn't Argentinean either. He was Portuguese. It seems like a strange thing to lie about today, but at that time in Jersey the local people, and a lot of my colleagues in the banking world, looked down on the island's Portuguese population who were there mostly as low-wage workers in the hotel and restaurant industries. 'Pork-and-cheese' and 'spic' were used casually and without conscience. Joe Santos. Originally the Portuguese and Spanish for 'saints'.

Saint. The irony of it makes me smile and wince at the same time. His behaviour. How his wife put up with him. My own self-absorption.

He said the Bolognese was great, he could tell I'd gone to a lot of trouble, but there was no way it would have been ready two hours earlier. No way.

Some things take time.

Hungry Writing Prompts 169 – 175

Write about a secret.

Write about someone who lied to you.

Write about a threat.

Write about the proof of love.

Write about the person you used to be.

Write about feeling sorry for yourself.

Write about something that takes time.

I ♥ Tomatoes

Not in a salad where their seeds and juice run into the leaves and make everything soggy but sliced and salted on a plate of their own and tumbled with fresh basil. Or cut into

chunks and cooked for a few minutes over a high heat in some olive oil with garlic, chilli and fresh chives and served on toast. Or stuffed with mince beef that's been simmered to a rich sauce with grated courgette and carrot, chopped tinned tomatoes, then topped with grated cheese and flashed under the grill. I like three large overlapping slices sprinkled with oregano on top of a cheese and potato pie. (Does anyone still make cheese and potato pie?) I like them picked from the vine and eaten while they're still warm from the sun. I like them sliced for an open tomato tart. I like sun-dried tomatoes, sun-blush tomatoes, green tomato chutney, home-made salsa.

My step-daughter grew this one – in fact she had three perfectly heart-shaped tomatoes from her father-in-law's greenhouse. John died last year, and the tomatoes felt like gifts from him, she said.

I don't believe in an afterlife, or any future rewards from a higher being. I don't believe the dead can speak to the living. But I do believe that the connections and relationships we create and experience while we're alive become a part of who we are. Acceptance, forgiveness, generosity, tolerance, resentment, rejection, selfishness, impatience. Perhaps the trick is to learn from them all and become the people we want to be.

SHEENA'S TOMATO TART

My friend, Sheena, who lives in France, showed me how to make this easy-peasy tart when we were staying with her and her husband Malcolm at their home near Toulouse. It's the perfect summer lunch, served with a green salad and a glass of chilled wine. Keen meat eaters might feel a little short-changed, but you could always satisfy them with a side plate of charcuterie. The black olives are my tweak, and I've also experimented with a layer of grated courgette directly under the layer of tomato, but if you do decide on that then make sure you dry the courgette thoroughly between sheets of kitchen paper, or you'll end up with a soggy everything, not just a bottom.

What you need:
- ☐ Ready-made pastry: puff, flaky or shortcrust as you prefer. (In France ready rolled pastry comes in circles, which makes perfect sense for tarts, while here in the UK you have to wrestle with and trim an oblong to fit your chosen dish. Brave heart, and all that.)
- ☐ A tablespoon of Dijon mustard, or to taste
- ☐ Grated cheese: Comté or Cheddar.
- ☐ Ripe tomatoes, sliced and with any tough core cut out.
- ☐ Pitted black olives.
- ☐ Olive oil
- ☐ Fresh or dried herbs: oregano, marjoram, or *herbes de provence* as you like
- ☐ Optional: a grated courgette, thoroughly dried in kitchen paper

What you do:
- ☐ Preheat the oven to Gas number 6 or 200°C
- ☐ Unroll the pastry with its baking parchment, and line a shallow dish, leaving the paper underneath. Trim the edges
- ☐ Prick the pastry base all over with a fork, as this helps avoid sogginess
- ☐ Spread the mustard over the base and top with the grated cheese
- ☐ (If you're using courgette add this now)
- ☐ Arrange the sliced tomatoes over the top, and decorate with the halved black olives
- ☐ Drizzle with olive oil
- ☐ Sprinkle with herbs and season with salt and pepper
- ☐ Bake for about 25 minutes, and check the pastry isn't getting too brown. 35 minutes is probably a maximum cooking time though
- ☐ Let it cool for 10 minutes or so to avoid burning the skin off your gums: we all know what hot tomatoes are like, and still we ignore it!

Hungry Writing Prompts 176 - 182

Write about what you love to eat.

Write about the warmth of the sun.

Write about an afterlife.

Write about gifts.

Write about something you really want to say to
a person in your life.

Write about a death in the family.

Write about a wake.

On Hunger

How to describe this feeling, this physical sensation that has settled below my solar plexus. It is like hunger in its hollowness, in my desire to feed it. Because what has been feeding

me for the last five days has left, travelling away from me here in Kent along the M4, crossing the bridge over the River Severn from England into Wales, past the old port cities along the coast towards the smoky clatter of plant and towers of a steelworks that announces Port Talbot, then turning south towards the sea. They're home. And what remains of them here are bright memories, like shadows stretching across sunlit grass.

My mam and dad, my niece, her husband and their two little kids have been staying with me. There have been darts and frisbees, footballs and bingo games. There have been walks and runs and falling over. Rabbits and deer. Sunrises and sunsets. There has been laughter. Lots of laughter. And there has been blackberry picking, pancake flipping, barbecuing and roasting, baking and wine pouring.

And now I find myself alone I am attempting to nourish that hollow feeling with a soup made with the home-grown tomatoes and red onions that Mam and Dad brought with them.

And then as I'm stirring the soup, my husband, Tony, calls from Corfu where the cruise ship he's lecturing and painting on has docked for the day, and his voice brings me home to myself, our life together.

We all need to be capable of feeding ourselves, but the nourishment we receive from the people in our life who we love, who love us, makes us whole.

Hungry Writing Prompts 183 – 189

Write about someone leaving.

Write about driving towards the coast.

Write about shadows.

Write about playing games.

Write about blackberry picking.

Write about a long distance telephone call.

Write about the people who make you whole.

MAM'S VEGETABLE SOUP

Nothing says 'nourishment' more to me more than this.

What you need:
- ☐ 1 medium onion, chopped
- ☐ 2 cloves of garlic, chopped or crushed
- ☐ 1 small swede, 1 large parsnip, 3 carrots, 3 small potatoes all finely diced (approximate amounts, as you should aim for an equal amount of each)
- ☐ 2 organic vegetable stock cubes
- ☐ 1 litre of water
- ☐ dried mixed herbs
- ☐ salt and pepper
- ☐ olive oil

What you do:
- ☐ Put all the veg and the olive oil in a large saucepan, cook for 10 mins, stirring occasionally
- ☐ Dissolve the stock cubes in boiling water and add to the vegetables with the herbs
- ☐ Simmer very gently for about 2 hours, and then season with salt and pepper to taste
- ☐ Sprinkle with freshly chopped parsley before serving

Why?

I once watched a woman striding down the main street of Santa Cruz, in California, with her shirt undone, her breasts on display. I didn't have a camera with me, but the scene is so alive in my memory – me inside the organic supermarket in the fruit and vegetable aisle and her walking past the open door in bright sunlight – that I could be looking at a film. It both surprised and disturbed me at the time, and that's undoubtedly the reason why I wrote the following poem. And after more than 20 years the memory retains those same reactions as if I still need answers to why she was doing this, and why on that street, and why she chose that day, that time.

Ripe Fruit

While I am choosing beefsteak tomatoes
in Good Earth I see her marching
down Pacific Avenue, bare breasts swinging.
She is laughing. I look down at my hands
their own two pounds of ripe fruit.

As she passes the store I see her breasts
are huge, humungous icing bags of flesh
but brown from the sun. Her skirt is blue

and long. Her open shirt flares in the breeze
rolling up Pacific from the sea.

There are police at the intersection.
Will they stop her there?
Will she help them bundle her breasts
back into the flimsy cotton of her shirt?
Will she resist them, or quietly watch

as they fumble with each one, embarrassed
at the weight in their hands threatening
to break free from the rickety clutch
of buttons? Will she still be laughing
or will she start to cry, wondering

why the morning had to come to this?

Hungry Writing Prompts 190 – 196

Write about a street you know well.

Write about being naked.

Write the story that precedes a familiar photograph.

Write about being ignored.

Write about a sea breeze.

Write about buttons.

Write about why you live the way you do.

Souvenirs

Pebbles. Shells. Postcards. That's what I normally bring back from a holiday. And the memories of newly discovered dishes. My trip to the Algarve last year saw me eating a small village's

quota of Portuguese Custard Tarts, and then I came home and made some of my own.

We were there, ostensibly, to play golf but I use the word 'play' in the loosest possible way – as a complete beginner I'd have had more success kicking the ball around the fairway. But, fortunately, there were plenty of tarts to comfort me afterwards. And a big, and I mean big, bath in our rented apartment to soak away the aches from muscles I didn't know I had.

'We could both fit in here,' I said to Tony, as the bath filled, the bubbles grew to a thick sparkling raft, and I started to tug off my clothes.

'What are you doing?' he said.

'Getting in,' I said.

'There's not enough room,' he said, admitting later that he was desperately trying to think of any reason to keep me out of it.

'There's loads of room!' I said. 'What are you talking about?'

'Look,' he said, frantically trying to dredge up another reason, 'I'm a big bloke and I just want to lie there with my legs open and relax.'

Three days later I was still laughing. I suppose you could say that after 30 years together romance hasn't just died, it's fossilised!

We were more in tune when we made the Portuguese Custard Tarts together. As lovely as they were I think filo pastry might be the way to go rather than puff, as the recipe we tried suggested. But I've never used filo. For some reason it scares me. It might be the warnings of it drying out easily that accompany any recipe that rec- ommends using it, of having to keep it between damp tea-towels. It sounds like high maintenance pastry. And I like recipes that are easy going, relaxing you might even say (as relaxing as you can get outside of a bath and with your legs firmly together!)

Hungry Writing Prompts 197 – 203

Write about beach-combing.

Write about something you bought on holiday.

Write about taking off your clothes.

Write about bubbles.

Write an obituary for the death of Romance.

Write about dryness.

Write about someone who is high-maintenance.

The Invention of 'Mousse'

What was your iconic party food as a child?

Mine was 'mousse': a whisked concoction of Rowntree's jelly and evaporated milk that my mother made. She filled stiff, waxed paper jelly dishes with it for birthday parties, glass dishes for Sunday teas, or used it to make a quick trifle topping, pouring it over the jelly-set Swiss roll and tinned fruit instead of the layers of custard and cream. After leaving it in the fridge for several hours it set around the million air bubbles added by a furious session with the rotary whisk. When you pushed your spoon in it made a sound that was a cross between a squeak (the noise jelly made) and a squelch (the noise of custard).

In a recent cloud of nostalgia I bought a new hand rotary whisk, a Faringdon 30cm 'Fouet rotatif' with stainless steel blades, but my mother still has and uses the same whisk she received as a wedding present over 60 years ago: a Prestige model with a dark wooden hand-rest and handle. It made the mousse, it beat eggs to a yellow cloud, and it took the lumps out of the gravy on Sunday morning if I'd added the potato water too quickly to the fat, flour and Oxo cubes.

But despite its usefulness, the rotary whisk (along with the other sharp and awkwardly shaped kitchen utensils: the silver carving knife, the potato peeler and masher, the turned metal skewers) was still one of the bad men in the country of Cutlery, the game I played in my head while wiping dishes. It was down to me, armed only with a tea-towel, to save the lives of the ordinary people: the knives and forks (fathers and mothers), teaspoons (the kids), and the deep-bowled tablespoons (grandmothers) who were so old and slow I was forever rescuing them at the last minute and delivering them to the safety of the cutlery drawer.

I believed the invention of mousse belonged to our family. No-one else's mother on our housing estate, let alone anywhere else in the country, made it. But in her book, *Miss Dahl's Voluptuous Delights*, Sophie Dahl gives a recipe for 'Clover's Carnation milk jelly' in honour of her younger sister. The brand of evaporated milk available at our local Co-op (pronounced 'kwop' in South Wales) was Ideal and I think that 'Ideal milk jelly' just caps Miss Dahl's pretty alliteration. Listen to the glee in its long second syllable and the conviction in its name: this milk really is the best.

IDEAL MILK JELLY
(aka Sandfields Estate Strawberry Mousse)

Sadly, I could not find Ideal evaporated milk in any supermarket, so I plumped for an 'own brand' rather than surrender to Carnation. You, of course, are not expected to display such staunch loyalty.

What you need:
- ☐ 1 packet of strawberry jelly
- ☐ half a large can of evaporated milk

What you do:
- ☐ Break up the jelly into a jug or bowl capable of holding at least 2 pints of liquid (the whisking will increase the quantity)
- ☐ Add enough boiling water to the jelly cubes to make half a pint, and stir until all the lumps dissolve, then leave it in the fridge until it begins to set. It'll probably take about half an hour, but you can tell it's ready when the jelly sticks to the sides of the bowl when you swish it around
- ☐ Set upon the jelly with the rotary whisk until it's very frothy then, in another larger bowl, whisk the evaporated milk to an equally frothy state
- ☐ Pour the jelly into the milk and whisk again until it's all one frothy homogenous mix
- ☐ Pour or scoop into jelly dishes and leave to set fully in the fridge for at least 2 to 3 hours

You can play with different flavoured jellies and make layers in glass dishes but make sure your bottom layer is firm enough before you add another or your mousse will be far from ideal … sorry, I couldn't resist!

Hungry Writing Prompts 204 – 210

Write about a tea party.

Write about sweetness.

Write about a wedding present.

Write about Sunday morning.

Write about something your mother made.

Write about someone who needs rescuing.

Write about loyalty.

Comfort
In memory of Lilian Lavinia Crosse 1920 – 1998

Tony's mother died unexpectedly in April 1998. She shouldn't have. She was fit and healthy. She told us she didn't want to 'bother anyone' when she started having breathing difficulties after somehow rupturing her oesophagus. Within two weeks the infection in her lung developed into toxaemia and she died.

Two years earlier she'd had a hip replacement, and stayed with us for a month to recuperate. During that time she went from sleeping upright in an armchair the week she came out of hospital to riding a bike for the first time in 60 years a few days before she went home.

Tony used to set her fitness goals, hiding lottery scratch cards in the hedge a little further along the lane each day. I tried to in-

crease the appetite she'd lost through so much pain prior to the operation, making the small and soft food I knew she liked: crust-less sandwiches, cod in parsley sauce. She used to say 'thank you' to me a dozen times a day.

Lilian Lavinia Crosse was born in 1920, and married in 1938. She had two sons before the end of the war then, 20 years later, when she was in her late 40s, a rather unexpected daughter. Tony remembers his dad, Jack, calling him at work in a wild panic
    'Son, it's your mother, your mother…'
    'What Dad, what is it?'
    'She's pregnant, son, and it can't be mine. I've only touched her once this year.'
    'That'll do it, Dad,' Tony said.

I'd only known Tony for a year when Jack died in the Summer of 1986.
    'When was your brother born?' I asked. We were getting all the official documentation together, birth certificate, marriage certificate, to take to the Registrar.
    'Um … February 1939.'
    'Your parents were only married in November 1938.'
    'The bugger!' Tony started to laugh. 'And he gave me and my brother such a hard time when we had to get married!'
    I was just amazed he hadn't already worked it out. His sister had. I had. I guess girls are like that.

Jack's funeral was a standard crematorium service. Tony chose two pieces of music, but apart from that we went along with everything the funeral director suggested. When Lil died twelve years later we wondered if we could do things differently. A copy of *The Dead Good Funerals Book* told us we could.
    We ordered a ready assembled cardboard coffin from Compakta Ltd, and Tony painted Lil's portrait at one end and a portrait of his dad at the other. On the sides he painted poppies and butterflies. Our lovely, local and centuries old, family funeral directors, Viners & Sons, collected it from our house the day before the funeral, went to the hospital to pick up Lil's body and then drove directly to the crematorium.

Lil wasn't religious, so we asked for all religious artefacts to be removed from the crematorium chapel, and declined the services of the chapel overseer in his priest-like robes. There was no organ, no dramatic journey of the coffin through a curtain. The only floral tributes were two arrangements of white lilies. Tony asked people, if they really wanted to contribute in some way, to send him a memory of Lilian, an anecdote or a photograph, something personal that reminded them of her.

I suppose we shouldn't have been surprised that people took offence, among them her older sister, a Catholic nun, who refused to attend. And I do understand that funerals should also be about comforting the living, but I am still glad we said goodbye to Lil in an informal and intimate way, a way she would have liked, and not have been frightened or intimidated by. I remember standing beside her after Jack's funeral, while everyone sombrely read the floral tributes and one of Jack's sisters wailed and threw herself across the bonnet of a car, and she clutched my arm and said, 'Lynne, get me out of here.'

So we sat beside her coffin for a while, read poems, swapped stories and laughed and cried. We took photographs of the tributes from her grandchildren, and Tony played the guitar and sang for her on the same date, 1st May, she'd given birth to him 54 years earlier.

Later, back at our house, we ate baked salmon and drank sweet sparkling wine because that's what Lil would have enjoyed. And we had a birthday cake for Tony who looked as if all the light had been wiped from his eyes, perhaps how all sons and daughters feel when the source that brought them into the world is extinguished.

What I remember most about her was her childlike perception of the world, how I never heard her say an unkind thing, and the incredible ease with which she laughed, with you and even more so at herself.

Towards the end of the month she spent with us we visited a neighbour's house for an early evening drink in their garden of classically laid out lawns and flower-beds.

'What I really like about your garden,' Tony said in conversation, 'is the symmetry.'

'Oh,' Lil said, 'have you got dead people buried here then?'

Hungry Writing Prompts 211 – 217

Write about riding a bike.

Write about soft food.

Write about a funeral.

Write about the songs that remind you of people
in your life.

Write about someone who takes offence.

Write about a birthday cake.

Write about burying something.

BAKED SALMON WITH CHILLI KICK LEEKS

What you need:
- ☐ 4 slim boneless salmon fillets
- ☐ 125g tub of cream cheese
- ☐ I garlic clove, crushed
- ☐ fresh breadcrumbs
- ☐ fresh grated parmesan
- ☐ fresh chopped parsley
- ☐ leeks
- ☐ butter and oil
- ☐ dried chillies

What you do:
- ☐ Mix the cream cheese with the crushed garlic, divide into four and spread over the salmon fillets
- ☐ Make fresh breadcrumbs (the hard way is to grate an uncut loaf, the easy way is to chuck a slice or two of wholemeal in your blender and blitz a few times) with grated fresh parmesan and freshly chopped parsley, or if you don't have any, you can use dried chives, add some pepper to taste, and press this mixture lightly all over the cheese topping
- ☐ Bake for 20 to 25 minutes at 200°C
- ☐ While the fish is cooking, finely slice three or four washed and dried leeks (not too much of the dark green bit) and sauté gently for around 5 to 8 minutes in a little oil and butter, adding 1 crushed dried piri-piri or bird's eye chilli for every two leeks.
- ☐ Serve the hot salmon on a bed of the soft, buttery leeks

And Then There Were Bees

Brett, the honey bee man, turned up at The Applehouse at 9am last Saturday. It was probably the dark green cargo pants and lighter green T-shirt that made me think 'Territorial Army' but he did have an authoritative, no-nonsense way about him too.

'I thought bees had to be transported at night,' I said.

'No,' he said. 'As long as it's cold enough.'

And cold enough it has been. We are renting beehives to help pollinate the apple trees in the orchard whose eruption of blossom is about a month later than usual this year. They're tucked in pairs beside the elder windbreaks, rather low on buzz quality, but Brett did say that they'd take a while to readjust to their new surroundings.

And he was right because a couple of days later there were hundreds of tiny brown bees surging in and out of the slot at the bottom of the hive. As Brett lives about 4 miles away there's no risk of the bees heading home: apparently 2 miles is the average distance that you have to move the hives to prevent them from doing that.

You'll have surely read that bees are in the news. 'One in three mouthfuls of the food we eat is dependent on pollination at a time when a crisis is threatening the world's honey bees', says the British Beekeepers' Association.

The Welsh Assembly government has taken steps to protect these essential pollinators but central government in Westminster has not taken any similar action and refused to support a ban of neonicotinoid chemicals in pesticides in 2013.

Our borrowed bees are safe: the land is virtually organic. But they are a microscopic part of the bee population in Kent, let alone in the UK. The EU has the power to restrict the usage of those chemicals despite the absence of a majority vote, and for our sake I hope that happens.

> If the bee disappeared off the face of the earth,
> man would only have four years left to live.
> Albert Einstein

In praise of honey bees I've made a cake that I last made 30 years ago, a statistic that makes me feel like Old Mother Hubbard! I made it as a dessert for one of the first Sunday lunches I cooked after I moved in with Tony in 1985. I'm trying to work out why I haven't bothered with it since, and I think I remember one half of it breaking in two when I tried to take it out of the tin which resulted in a mini nervous breakdown complete with tears. I wanted to do everything so perfectly in those early days.

Happily, there wasn't even a cake-scrape of stress involved in yesterday's baking session. Even when Tesco's shelves were bare of blanched hazelnuts. I bought the chopped and roasted ones instead. You do need a grinder attachment on your food processor for this recipe, as the hazelnuts need to be ground, and I've yet to see them on supermarket shelves. Or you can use a coffee grinder, or robust biceps and a big pestle and mortar. I have an ancient electric coffee grinder that I keep for grinding small quantities of spices and nuts ... the same grinder I used for the first time 30 years ago.

(4-6) Hazelnut Meringue Cake.

4 Egg whites . 8 tbsp clear honey
   8oz grond hazelnuts

Filling — 1/4 pt dable cream
          icing sugar to dust.

Whisk egg whites until stiff.
Gradually trickle in honey whisking
continuasly + continue whisking
until stiff + glossy.
Fold in grond hazelnuts.

Line. 2 8" sandwich tins with non-
stick baking parchment.
Divide mixture between 2 tins +
bake MK4 for 40 mins.

Turn one meringue onto serving plate
remove lining + allow to cool

Whip cream until stiff + spread over cake.
Turn out 2nd meringue, remove paper
+ carefully place on top.
Sprinkle over icing sugar. (in doily shape
(if you like)

HAZELNUT AND HONEY MERINGUE CAKE

If you're wheat intolerant then this is a cake for you: no flour. No fat either. Or sugar, at least not in its sprinkly form.

The only change I made to the original recipe, whose provenance has been lost in the intervening years, was adding some Grand Marnier to the double/heavy cream before whipping it up for the filling. The next time I make it – which will have to be before another 30 years passes or I won't be able to bend down and get the damn thing in the oven – I'm going to try coffee flavoured cream.

It's a cake that shouts 'afternoon tea'. It has both sweetness and lightness; it makes me think of doilies and antimacassars and bone china plates and cake forks. But it was only a doily that got anywhere near my attempt. I placed a small paper one on the top, planning to dust icing sugar over it and create a pretty pattern. But the sugar fell out of the jar and through the sieve in such a quantity I didn't quite get the effect I was after. More avalanche than light dusting. But it still tasted good.

Hungry Writing Prompts 218 – 224

Write about the sound of bees.

Write about cold weather.

Write about disappearing.

Write about perfection.

Write about what you will do in the years you have left to live.

Write about something that happened 30 years ago.

Write about delicacy.

Come Into the Parlour

I n Wales this week to research for my book, *Real Port Talbot*, I have three visits lined up: a forest, the deep water docks and the mayor's parlour. Don't you love the word 'parlour'? From the French *parler* – to speak — and originally used for a room set aside for receiving and speaking to people. So that's spot on for the Mayor's room in the Civic Centre. Although the phrase, 'The Mayor's Parlour' makes me think of plumpness and chortling: overstuffed chairs and waistcoats stretched over jiggling bellies.

Parlours had their day in both grand and much less grand homes. My parents' house in Port Talbot, South Wales was built in 1957 with two downstairs reception rooms: the living room at the back of the house, the hub of everyday life, and the front room, which we called the parlour. The parlour was kept for best and, as we grew up, where my sister and I sat with our boyfriends in the evenings in separate chairs on opposite sides of the gas fire. No hanky-panky in the parlour, thank you!

The parlour was where we had this early family portrait taken. I remember those faint leaves floating up the skin of the wallpaper like ghosts. The green patterned carpet had just been laid: you can make out a cut-off in the background. It was 1964 and we are the perfect advertisement for a crease-free family: Courtelle, Bri-Nylon, Crimplene.

It must have been a year or two later on Christmas Day that my sister and I sneaked downstairs just after dawn to discover there were no presents in front of the gas fire in the living room where they'd always been.

With our hearts as tight as clenched fists we looked in the kitchen, the porch, and then found them in the parlour and, in prize of place, a large dolls' house my dad had made, the roof papered with brick printed wallpaper. Slowly, and with some difficulty, we carried it into the living room, then went back to shift the rest of the presents too.

'But we put them in there so you'd have more room and there'd be less mess in here,' my mother said when she got up and found us in a sea of wrapping paper in the living room. But the parlour wasn't where we lived, where we ate and watched TV. That room was for unfamiliar things.

The division is not so obvious now. The wall between the front room and the hallway was demolished making an open plan space with the staircase in the corner. It has the dining table and chairs in it, the same set my parents bought after their marriage in 1952. There's an oak and stained glass bookcase from my paternal grandfather's house, and a computer desk for my mother's laptop and printer. We eat in here when there are more than three of us at home. We cut my parents' anniversary cakes in here. My great niece and nephew dance in here when they visit. Lulu's 'Shout' is a favourite. This is where we play board games. My mother keeps any flowers she has in this room because it's cooler than the living room which faces south-west. And it's always the front-room now, never the parlour. But there's still a sense of otherness about it, as if it's been set aside for possibilities, not the business of everyday, ordinary living.

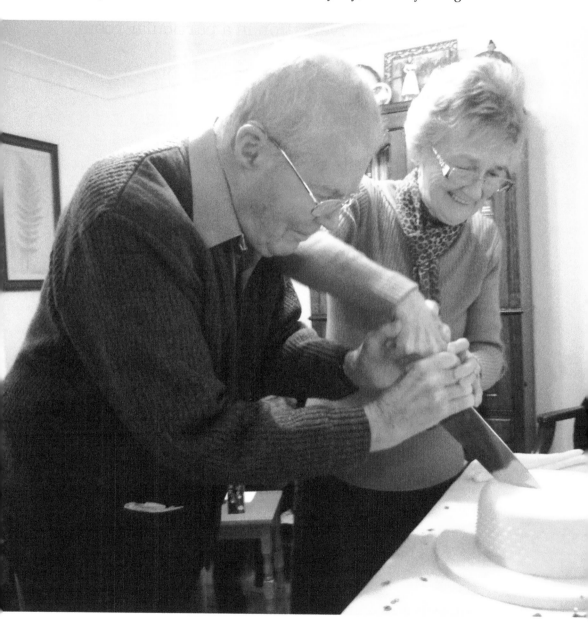

Hungry Writing Prompts 225 – 231

Write about something quintessentially British.

Write about a conversation in a particular room.

Write about a family portrait.

Write about Christmas morning.

Write about searching.

Write about an anniversary.

Write about the business of everyday living.

The Taste of Life

I n Aimee Bender's *The Particular Sadness of Lemon Cake,* nine-year-old Rose tastes emotions in the food she eats:

> So every food has a feeling, George said when I
> tried to explain to him the acid resentment in the
> grape jelly.
> I guess, I said. A lot of feelings, I said.

When she tastes her brother's toast, with butter and jam and sprinkles of sugar, she detects something folding in on itself. At the bakery she tastes the baker's tight anger in a chocolate chip cookie.

I always taste expectation in the first few sips of champagne. Burnt pizza tastes like meanness. The hot, fluffy flesh of a jacket potato is somewhere between laughter and sleep.

All the dinners I resisted eating when I was little: could I taste my mother's hard work and thrift in them? I was too young to empathise with the effort required for her to keep a house, to feed and clothe three kids, to pay the rent and bills on my dad's steelworker's wage, and still put away a little each week. I am sure she went without for us. I am sure they both did.

When I was eleven I visited the Roman Baths in Bath, grown up enough to wander around the thermal spa ahead of my parents, old enough to have my own pocket money to spend in the Pump Room tea and coffee shop.

It was sitting in its own fluted white paper case, and looked like a large doughnut glazed with syrup; a flower of cream had been nozzled onto its crown. Its exotic name was hand-written on a folded card: *Rum Baba*. It had to be delicious.

Even with the first mouthful the cloying sweetness seemed to penetrate my teeth and gums while another flavour, probably rum essence rather than real rum, rushed like a wave of acrid disappointment to the back of my throat, my nose, and even into my eyes. These were flavours beyond the capabilities of my young taste buds. This was a cake from an adult world. It repelled and confused me. And I felt like crying when I left it, uneaten, on the table, the proof of my pocket money squandered.

The spa water at the Roman baths was laced with minerals: it made us smack our tongues against our teeth, the roofs of our mouths. Is this what the past tastes like? Layers of salts and sulphur compounds, calcium, potassium, magnesium. Fissures and pathways. Hardness and softness.

Hungry Writing Prompts 232 – 238

Write about sadness.

Write about food that makes you happy.

Write about sleep.

Write about the things your parents never had.

Write about someone eating cake in a coffee shop.

Write about crying in a public place.

Write about hardness.

Let's Do Breakfast

Are you a black coffee and a cigarette? Three cups of tea? Juice and toast? A bowl of cereal? Full English? Or a Full Welsh – with laverbread and/or cockles? Kippers? One of the tastiest breakfasts I ever had was at the Gwesty Cymru Hotel in Aberystwyth, North Wales. A poached egg and thick cut bacon on a slice of Welsh Rarebit.

I don't poach eggs at home. They make me nervous. I am never sure there'll be no sloppy white inside until I cut them open and then all I can do is shiver. If anyone has a foolproof way of cooking them to a firm white and runny yolk then please, please let me know.

So scrambled is my fall-back process at home: with a good dollop of crème fraiche added towards the end of cooking to keep them creamy, a sprinkling of chopped chives and, when I have them in the bread bin, dry-fried croissant slices.

In his book, *At Home*, Bill Bryson describes a breakfast eaten by the Duke of Wellington (1769–1852): 'two pigeons and three beef steaks, three parts of a bottle of Moselle, a glass of champagne, two glasses of port and a glass of brandy.' Maybe you need to have a battle scheduled for the day to really want to pack that lot into your belly.

My *Mrs Beeton's Book of Household Management* from 1912 lists a menu for a Simple Breakfast in Winter: *Cream of Wheat, Scrambled Eggs, Fried Bacon, Brawn, Baked Apples, Scones, Toast, Bread, Butter, Jam, Tea, Coffee, Hot and Cold Milk.* Yep, that's simple! Because there wasn't always the time to tackle the Family Breakfast menus that included: grilled kidneys, baked halibut steaks, cold ham, croquettes of fish, fried whiting, veal cake, sausages and game pie.

Someone asking you to drop a slice of bread into the toaster and pass the jam out of the fridge pales into insignificance, doesn't it?

Mrs Beeton believed that "the moral and physical welfare of mankind depends largely on its breakfast". Hmmm… It's the kind of statement that makes you wonder what Attila the Hun, Hitler, Gandhi and Mother Theresa ate for breakfast. However, when she says, "A being well fed and warmed is naturally on better terms with himself", that makes perfect sense to me. I get grumpy when I'm hungry.

Mrs Beeton also has lots of sage advice about laying the breakfast table: what cutlery to provide, where the serviette might be positioned, where on the table any cold dishes should be placed. It's a minefield. Fortunately there are "no hard-and-fast rules … for the disposal of the cruets, butter, toast, eggs, marmalade". That's a relief. The times I've stood over the breakfast table with a salt pot and butter dish deliberating over where to put them.

Hungry Writing Prompts 239 - 245

Write about a hotel breakfast.

Write about the things that unsettle you.

Write about a battle.

Write about someone's morals.

Write about being grumpy.

Write about rules, what you will and will not do.

Write about laying a table.

The Scent of Memory

How do you describe the smell of rain to someone? Or the scent that rises from a drawer full of fresh but worn bed linen when you first open it? I have been trying to articulate the smell of my dad's black donkey jacket, the one he wore to work in the 1960s. When he came home from his shifts at the steelworks he hung it under the stairs in the porch. The closest I can get is a mixture of engine oil, cold weather and the inside of a lorry cab.

Tony bought some cheese a couple of weeks ago, two white Stiltons, one with chopped mango the other with blueberries. I couldn't eat the first one: it tasted like tomcats to me.

'Don't be so ridiculous!' he said.

'I know what you mean!' his daughter said.

Not that either of us, please believe me, have tasted any part of a tom cat but there was something about the acidity, the sourness, that automatically conjured the image in my head. Or in my mouth.

There's a poem by Kate Clanchy called, 'Poem for a man with no sense of smell' that closes with:

> the delicate hairs on the nape
> of my neck …

hold a scent so frail and precise as a fleet
of tiny origami ships, just setting out to sea.[4]

If you asked me to I would try and articulate why that makes sense to me, but it feels right before I even begin to think about it. Intimacy and fragility: there's a connection there that makes intuitive sense.

I can't imagine anyone without a sense of taste wanting to try the stilton with mango after I tell them it tastes like tomcats. But maybe you would want to try a slice of *Bara Brith* if I told you it tasted like the smell of dark fruit puddings maturing in white bowls on pantry shelves, that slicing it evokes a memory of the sea, of herding salt and peppery piles of sand into piles along the windowsill in a childhood bedroom. That it looks how the word *cariad* (beloved) makes you feel when someone you love says it to you. And I'd hope you wouldn't be disappointed if you experienced none of those things.

---

4 from *Slattern*, Chatto & Windus, 1995

BARA BRITH (SPECKLED BREAD)

The traditional recipe appears in *Favourite Welsh Recipes*[5] but I've tweaked it: I use a mix of sultanas and raisins (not currants), ordinary black tea (I've tried Earl Grey because I thought it might complement the lemon rind, but it isn't tea-y enough for me), a mix of white and wholemeal flour so it's a little lighter, and ground nutmeg when I haven't had mixed spice to hand.

What you need:
- ☐ 10 oz mixed dried fruit
- ☐ two thirds of a pint of hot tea
- ☐ 3 oz soft brown sugar
- ☐ grated rind of 1 lemon
- ☐ 12 oz self-raising wholemeal flour
- ☐ 1 teaspoon mixed spice
- ☐ 1 large egg

What you do:
- ☐ Soak the mixed fruit in hot tea, cover and leave to stand overnight
- ☐ Set oven at Gas Mark 4 or 350 F and grease and line a 2 lb loaf tin
- ☐ Strain fruit, reserving liquid, and mix with other ingredients, adding a little of the reserved liquid to achieve a soft dropping consistency
- ☐ Pour into tin and bake for about 45 to 55 minutes
- ☐ Test to see if it's cooked by plunging a skinny wooden skewer into the middle: if it comes out sticky give it another five minutes. You can cover the top with baking parchment if it's getting too brown

It has a kind of bendy/rubbery feel to it when it first comes out of the oven which makes it difficult to slice until it's cool. But it is so lovely spread with unsalted butter when it's still a little warm so it's worth tackling the rubberiness and cutting off one end, and a slice or two.

---

5   Compiled by Sheila Howells and published by J Salmon Ltd., UK

Hungry Writing Prompts 246 – 252

Write about the sound of rain.

Write about the scent of bed linen.

Write about your father.

Write about cats.

Write about something glimpsed on the horizon.

Write about sand.

Write about the things that remind you of love.

Can I Tell You Something?

The gap between my lukewarm lasagne going back to the kitchen at the local Beefeater, and a hot, freshly prepared one replacing it is gratifyingly filled with the chatter of my 8-year-old great-niece, Ffion, each revelation prefaced by:

'Lynne?'

'Ffion?'

'Can I tell you something?'

☐ A woman on TV who was 101 remembered her little brother being born when she was three. This was her furthest [sic] memory.

☐ When I was in school did other children pick me up? Hannah, her friend, keeps picking her up and she doesn't like it.

☐ She is four foot tall.

☐ She didn't really want to

be eight but she didn't really like being seven.

☐ Mr Doyle, the headmaster, is retiring in July.

☐ She has three money boxes: one Principality and two Hello Kitties.

☐ She is upset with Mittens who scratched Tickles' nose through the bars of his cage.

☐ She scored the winning goal when Emma tripped.

☐ Iwan doesn't want to go to Bristol Zoo because of the peacocks.

☐ A newt ran into Miss Trunchbull's knickers.

All this and more for the bargain price of £1 – a Beefeater special for kids who eat with adults between 3pm and 5pm. And my replaced lasagne was pretty good too.

Now, after dropping off Ffion, I am in my parents' house looking through the window of my childhood bedroom. I watch the mist slip in from the sea, veiling the promenade's railings, the waste land in front of Tirmorfa Road, then nudging the greenhouses at the bottom of Mam and Dad's garden. The cries of seagulls are muted, the sea a soft rumble.

My 'furthest' memory? Either a yellow dress, bright sunlight and falling against the concrete step outside the back door and cutting open my chin, or sitting in a sandpit at the bottom of the garden, the sand cool and damp against the back of my bare legs.

Hungry Writing Prompts 253 – 259

Write about something hot.

Write about a bargain.

Write about the view from your window.

Write about mist or fog.

Write about your 'furthest' memory.

Write about what you find at the bottom of a garden.

Write about damp skin.

I Dream About Food

Spiced lamb samosas for a dinner party of 12 until
my friend says that at least three or four guests are
vegetarian. What about the others? I ask her. Do
they eat red meat? I don't think so, she says. And
there's less than an hour before everyone arrives.
We could go and get fish and chips, I suggest. But
now I don't want to be the one in charge. I don't
want to face these disappointed and disagree-
able people. And I tell her: if they're invited to

someone's house for dinner they shouldn't refuse to eat what they're served. That's just plain bad manners. I'm losing in all directions: my food, my friends, my generosity of spirit.

call these 'fish-hook dreams': ones that weigh heavily in me when I wake up and threaten to tug me along by the lip for the rest of the day if I let them. But I don't have to let them. I just have to recognise that my emotional response has been produced by the dream's wake. I can keep my head above the water; I don't have to go under.

This morning the lawn is spiked with tiny mushrooms.

I watch their caps soften and stretch like Dali's soft watches until they're just a smear of their former selves. Mushroom identification, on the web, is more challenging than I thought it would be but, as far as I can tell, these are *Coprinopsis atramentaria* – common ink caps – which are poisonous when consumed with alcohol. No

Wild Mushroom Tarlets, from BBC Good Food: http://www.bbcgoodfood.com/recipes/4757/wild-mushroom-tartlets

danger of that happening: they're not the most appetising looking fungi around, particularly as they slip towards their demise. But I'm grateful to them for introducing me to the charming word 'deliquescence': to dissolve gradually by absorbing moisture from the atmosphere; to melt away. But as beautiful as it is I can't imagine ever using it in a line of prose or poetry; words with their roots in Old English, like melt and soften, feel more comfortable in my mouth, sound more authentic in my voice on the page.

But let's stay with mushrooms. More specifically Mushroom Tartlings. (Or 'tartlets' if you're from the BBC or just prefer proper words.) I use these loose-bottomed tins, prick the base of the pastry with a fork and pile in the mushroom mixture. That way there's less of a puff pastry frame to munch your way through.

They are lovely, sweet and meaty in a non-meaty way. So why didn't I think of these in my dream for the wanting vegetarians and unfairly judged non-red meat eaters? I could have saved myself all that angst. Kept my friends. But it usually involves a morsel of pain, a sprinkling of regret for not knowing better sooner, for me to learn something. In dreams and in waking life.

Hungry Writing Prompts 260 – 266

Write about losing a friend.

Write about drowning.

Write about the early morning.

Write about poison.

Write about melting away.

Write about saving yourself.

Write about a lesson learned.

Feeling Sure

We need that, don't we? To feel sure of people we are close to? A surety that allows us to trust them, feel safe. Or just feeling sure that even breached by many years, the next

time you meet your conversation will be a continuation: renewed, an easiness settling around you.

We probably all have friends like that. Ones we might go months without seeing. Others who live in different countries that we might not see for years and years.

Some almond and chocolate beauties arrived in the post today from our friends in St Pere de Riudebitlles, a village north west of Barcelona. They're called *Catanies*, a Catalan speciality from the nearby town of Vilafranca del Penedes. We haven't seen Engracia and Enric, and their sons Darwin and Gerard, for over 12 years. But between 1994 and 1995, when we were living in Barcelona, we spent most of our days with them. Tony made huge sheets of paper on the terrace of their house, as part of his Masters in European Fine Art, using paper pulp from the factory they ran then and their sons run today.

Enric had handed Tony the keys to their house the first day they met, when Tony turned up at the factory to ask if he could buy some pulp for his work. Enric refused any payment and said, 'You can work here.'

Engracia fed us. She made stacks of tortillas – plain, garlic and parsley, and potato. At Christmas she gave us gambas cooked in sherry and a leg of lamb slow roasted on a bed of sweet onions. When they were in season she prepared *calçots*, a green onion that resembles a long baby leek, grilling them on the outdoor barbecue and serving them to us with a romesco dipping sauce made from ground almonds. On Sunday mornings I walked to the *Polleria* with her to buy spit roasted chickens and potatoes that had cooked in the fat dripping from the crisping birds.

When we left to come home in June 1995 we said goodbye to them in the courtyard of the paper factory, seven year old Gerard pointing at me and laughing, 'Why is she crying?', while his parents hushed him and blinked back their own tears.

I don't care if all this sounds sentimental. I want to remember and record that special relationship between me and Tony and Enric and Engracia. It was unspoken and unexamined. But somehow we felt sure of each other. And it remains like that. That's a gift that cannot be measured. One to always treasure.

Hungry Writing Prompts 267 – 273

Write about what's sure in life.

Write about the beginning of a conversation.

Write about a gift received in the post.

Write about an instantaneous connection with someone or something.

Write about a child laughing.

Write about a memorable meal in another country.

Write about something that can't be measured.

First Times

My great-nephew Harri celebrated his first Christmas last year. I'm sure he enjoyed the unexpected glitter and rustle, the fuss and attention of his extended family. But he won't remember the event that his parents have branded on their memories with a love and pride they never thought possible before his arrival in the world.

I've always imagined that we don't remember the earliest moments of our lives as babies and toddlers because it would be neural overload to remember all, or even some, of those new experiences, all those stimulating, enticing and sometimes frightening 'first times'. How could we possibly process so much novelty at such a rapid pace: the sounds and sights, the sensory explosions of tastes and textures that create a world we begin to catalogue and recognise? But the science is rather more complex.[6] It's possibly a storage failure and that we do retain all those individual fragments of information but our brains don't develop the ability to bundle all those fragments together and create memories before the age of between two and four. Or it's a retrieval issue: our perception of the world changes as we grow up so the cues associated with our earliest memories (e.g. furniture towering over us) are no longer

---

6 http://brainconnection.brainhq.com/2013/04/22/gone-but-not-forgotten-the-mystery-behind-infant-memories/

present. And we also have a memory system that's divided into the conscious recollection of experience and unconscious memories of skills and habits. There's a lot going on behind those wide open eyes.

Of course we don't lose the experience of 'first times' as we get older. But it's easy to lose, or dilute, our spontaneous responses. So it's good to remind ourselves to express joy and delight and surprise when they manifest in our lives.

The whole of the newly planted apple orchard was festooned with spider webs one morning. Not just one or two trees, but dozens and dozens of them along three whole rows. If there was ever a way to describe feeling trapped inside the good bit of a fairy tale then this was it. Has it been happening the whole of my life but I had to wait more than 50 years to experience it? If so, it was more than worth it.

Sometimes I have to look at photographs to remind me of the glory of a new experience. The downsides of adult living – ill-health, grief, anxiety – can get in the way of being open to joy. But each day is new. A whole 24 hours of never lived before-ness.

Little Harri does not know this yet. He doesn't need to. But his eyes are wide open, his face lit with a smile or creased with a frown. Hello world, he says even before the beginning of words.

Hungry Writing Prompts 274 – 280

Write about something that glitters.

Write about a memory you only partially remember and invent the rest.

Write about a spider's web.

Write about your favourite character from a fairy tale.

Write about what gets in the way of joy.

Write about a new day.

Write about having no words.

The Great British Bakery

It is just before nine on a Friday morning and while I wait for my car to be serviced at a local garage I have tucked myself behind the bakery's corner table next to a chiller cabinet that growls intermittently like a reluctant tractor, with a bacon bap and a milky coffee, the foam swirled and peaked like a cloud and thick enough to eat with a spoon, the only customer here.

And then it begins: a clutch of mothers returning from the school run, men in work boots or jangling keys, one man with a swept back wave of silvered hair who beams, 'Helloah!' into his mobile as he pushes through the door, another with a damp umbrella, some office workers, according to my opinion of their shoes. Like a flood erupting into the warmth and light from the dull and drizzled street.

Farmhouse, cottage, bloomer: seeded, granary and rye. Bread pudding, Belgian buns, cherry Bakewell tarts with bright red noses. Lemon drizzle cake and carrot cake and Eccles cakes, and doughnuts filled with vanilla and jam. And sausage rolls, bacon wrapped in pastry blankets, pasties, cheese twists. And the garish wonder of a tray baked Tottenham cake dressed in pink icing with a quilt of sugar strands. I listen as a Sandwich loaf rumbles towards its destiny of thinly sliced.

And no sooner does one flood recede then another one builds.

Paper bags and white cake boxes lifted over the glass cabinets like babies.

We talk of holidays in France, recall the bread, the hypnotic windows of patisseries, their gleaming, surgically precise cakes decorated like carnival floats and Ascot hats. But on a grey British day it's comfort we're after: pillowed packets of rolls soft enough to dream on, the almost unbearable sweetness of a Gypsy Tart, a jammy shortbread heart.

Hungry Writing Prompts 281 - 287

Write about being the only person in a room.

Write about clouds.

Write about a loaf of bread.

Write about a carnival or fairground.

Write about a flood.

Write about a grey day.

Write about a heart that's been soured.

Daily Bread

When I first encountered bagels on a supermarket shelf for the first time, in Florida in the summer of 1988, I was impressed by their versatility: plain, onion, poppy seeded, something very speckled (this could have been what I've since discovered is called 'Everything') and cinnamon and raisin. This is a bread roll that knows how to compete, I thought. A bread roll that goes the distance.

It was Andrea, the wife of British artist, Barry Leighton Jones, who we were living with that summer, who introduced them to me: lightly toasted, spread with cream cheese, draped with smoked salmon, and crowned with sliced red onion and tomato. That's tomahto not tomayto.

Cream cheese and smoked salmon on toast is nice but it doesn't compare with a bagel, its hint of resistance when you first bite, before your teeth sink into the doughy interior. This is dough that persists, pushes and wraps into every crevice in your mouth. But no-one can resist softness, pliability; it would be just too damn rude to complain, rather like criticising champagne for its bubbles.

When I eat them now, I always remember that surprising, life-expanding summer of citrus trees in the garden, a swimming pool the temperature of a warm bath, flash rain storms that could turn a parking lot into a lake within minutes. And tree frogs and mosquitoes. And the first words I ever wrote, the beginning of myself as a writer.

How can a simple bread roll be capable of reviving such rich memories, such deep emotion? Maybe because it's something that's intrinsic to our life experience, the ordinary (in its place in the past and present kitchens of our imaginations) and the reverential ('Give us this day our daily bread'). And it is capable of such weight too, such significance: hunger and revolution, fairy tales and the terrible truth of history.

Here's an excerpt from my book, *forgiving the rain*, about bread, about its power and its glory:

> At school and at Sunday-school I closed my eyes, clasped my hands together and prayed in English and Welsh: Give us this day our daily bread: *Dyro i ni heddiw ein bara beunyddiol*, words I repeated by rote that meant nothing to me.
>
> It came to us in a van that toured the estate street by street whose back doors opened to slatted shelves and the smell of flour, where I gazed at the plump Cottage loaves and imagined carrying one home in my arms like a baby. But I always parted with the half-crown piece for the disappointingly smooth, pale crust of a Sandwich Loaf that my mother would slice with a silver knife.
>
> At mealtimes, unless there was gravy on our plates, it sat in the middle of the table – bread and butter, *bara menyn* – thin slices, cut in half, which we were expected to eat, out of habit, tradition, a memory of hunger.

What are your memories of bread? The crusts, the crumbs?

Hungry Writing Prompts 288 – 294

Write about meeting someone for the first time.

Write about persistence.

Write about the beginning of yourself.

Write about praying.

Write about a knife.

Write about being hungry.

Write about crumbs.

Daring to Know My Manchego with Immanuel Kant

One of the things I learned (and re-learned) while writing about my Welsh hometown in *Real Port Talbot* was: beware of what you think you know. Several times I was aware of my preconceptions of a place contradicting what I was newly discovering; several times I had to remind myself to approach a place like a curious stranger not a familiar (and judgemental) local. There's no surprise for a mind that's already mapped and staked the ground.

And I've just read this:

> Daring to know requires daring to admit what we don't. It also means daring to accept that some of what we have most firmly believed to be true may not be so after all.

It's from Julian Baggini's book, *The Virtues of the Table: How to Eat and Think*, where philosophy meets the pleasure of eating and 'the riddles and dilemmas and contradictions surrounding the food on our plates'.

It's not just a thinking feast, though. Or a thinking nightmare if the idea of applying philosophy to the day to day experiences of food fills you with dread. He tags on loose recipes at the end of every section: I'm only on page 36 and I've nibbled from an inspiring cheeseboard and followed that up with a vegetable risotto and apple and blackberry crumble.

And already his ideas have pushed a few of my buttons and made me rethink what I thought I thought. How about this: buying food that's travelled by container ship from China could be a better choice than food driven through the UK. At least as far as carbon footprints are concerned. His arguments and ideas concerning currently popular terms like organic, local, sustainable, free range, Vegetarian Society approved and even PDO – Protected Designation of Origin – are thought provoking. And damn annoying. Who said thinking for yourself would be easy though?

But I am grateful that one of my favourite cheeses, Manchego, made from sheep's milk, comes out with one green flag that matters a lot to me: sheep are not intensively reared, so animal welfare isn't a major issue here.

Sapere aude. Dare to think. The philosopher Immanuel Kant's words. And now for one of those delightful ways that some subjects segue very satisfyingly into each other: an excess of cheese may have contributed to Kant's high blood pressure, his stroke and subsequent death. His last words have been reported as *Es ist gut* about the bread and wine his friend and biographer, E.A.C. Wasianski, had served him. You have to admire a man who enjoys his food right until the end.

Hungry Writing Prompts 295 – 301

Write about something you used to believe but don't anymore.

Write about being dared to do something.

Write about someone's last words.

Write about the map of your life.

Write about a long journey.

Write about cheese.

Write about what is good.

It's Breakfast, Jim, But Not as We Know It

Well, did you ever? And do you now? Spread one (or two) Weetabix with butter and jam, like a crisp-bread, or a slice of toast?

It came back to me this morning, a childhood memory of spreading welsh butter and strawberry jam on one in my mother's kitchen. I can't remember if it was breakfast time, or when I came home from school in the afternoon. If it was breakfast time perhaps we were short of milk … but that doesn't feel right. Milk was delivered in red foil topped bottles to our back door every morning. I do remember the effortful gum-sticking process of chewing through it: both butter and jam overwhelmed by the dryness of a biscuit that lodged between every tooth and resisted the concerted dislodging efforts of my tongue for hours afterwards.

This morning I used unsalted French butter and home-made blackberry and apple jam, more generously, I am sure, than my 10 year old self would have dared. And the memory is remade, but differently, as I eat every mouthful with ease and pleasure.

At the same time this feels like more than re-experiencing a taste of childhood: it feels it could be about culture and economy too. About a working class family who managed and got by thanks to hard work, thrift and invention. I might be teetering on the edge of melodrama and sentimentality, imbuing a simple Weetabix with that back-story, but the objects of our lives, from food and possessions, toys and clothes, the things we preserve and throw away, contain the stories of our lives.

And Weetabix have certainly played a part in all our stories: from its creation in 1932, through WWII and rationing, and export to Canada and the USA in the late 1960s. 3D technology, space travel, Dr Who, polar expeditions: yep, Weetabix came with us. Take a look for yourself on their website's History page[7] for a fascinating 81 years of social and manufacturing history.

But it seems I am not as original as I thought: back in 1939 Weetabix was 'making a man' of a small boy on a trike. And how? Spread with butter and jam.

---

7   http://www.weetabix.co.uk/weetabix-food-company/history

Hungry Writing Prompts 302 – 308

Write about yourself as a child.

Write about coming home from school.

Write about having more.

Write about breakfast.

Write about the objects you remember in your
parents' house.

Write about having less.

Write about a boy and the man he becomes.

Eating Cake with Sir Edmund Hillary

'How about a Kendal Mint Cake?' asks the woman in Outdoor World, Porthmadog, North Wales. I'm leading a 'Writing in the Landscape' course at the nearby writers' centre, Ty Newydd, and have come here in search of waterproof trousers.

'No thanks,' I say. 'I don't like the idea of mint-flavoured cake.'

I'm due a 60p refund on an exchange of women's trousers that could have seen me and the Andrews Sisters wearing them all at once, (and dancing), for a pair that the packet says fits 11/12-year-olds. All I can say is, they breed 'em big in North Wales.

I tell her not to worry about the refund. 'Put it in the charity box when you cash up,' I say. But she can't, the 'system' doesn't allow for that.

'You've paid for it so you might as well try it now,' she says, handing me one. Then, 'You're not diabetic, are you?'

I needn't have worried about the 'cake' because it's not cake at all as I'm sure a lot of you already know. Committed hikers and climbers are now probably all shaking their heads in despair because they wolf down these darlings with enthusiasm. But only because that's the last thing remaining at the bottom of their rucksack after being stranded on a hail-scarred mountainside for 72 hours, and it's either that or your fellow climber's arm. Just kidding.

If I had been a diabetic then I should have been worried. The quantity of sugar and glucose syrup in one of these bars makes your gums ache with even the smallest of slices. Not that they slice that well. They shatter.

But they do soften surprisingly quickly in your mouth. Think After Eight Mint on steroids and you'll get a pretty good idea of their texture and taste. And enjoyable in small amounts. I'd be happy to share my bar, in the event of a desperate food shortage, with at least three others.

And the link to Sir Edmund?

Romney's, a mint cake manufacturer in Cumbria since 1936, were asked in 1953 if they could quickly come up with enough mint cake to supply the Everest expedition to allow Sir Edmund Hillary and Sirdar Tensing to munch their way through an unspecified amount while they battled for the summit.

And in honour of Sir Edmund here's a little icy cliff face of Kendal Mint Cake for you to climb in your imaginations.

See those specks of chocolate? You're nearly at the top, keep going.

Hungry Writing Prompts 309 – 315

Write about giving something away.

Write about what's too big for you.

Write about too much sweetness.

Write about not having enough to eat.

Write about being caught in a storm.

Write about sharing.

Write about climbing a mountain.

First Crop

Dad's first crop of runner beans, picked today, topped and tailed and strung, ribbon sliced and cooked 'al dente', seasoned with butter and pepper. They are the taste of 1960s' childhood summers in South Wales, of the scent of caterpillars and

cabbage leaves on my fingers, sunburn and prickly heat, the pink cracks of calamine lotion on my skin, shell gardens assembled in sand-filled fruit boxes, rose petals soaking for days in water and hope, the three-legged race, a dirndl skirt in turquoise seersucker never completed in the last year of Junior school, a new leather satchel, Tuff shoes.

The years compress: a squeeze box of sounds, some as distant as echoes, others like the ringing of a school bell demanding attention.

And this one now that arrives like a breeze: a purple swimsuit with a red stripe, the sun beating on my shoulders, the sand hotter than burnt toast, and the sea so far out I think I might never reach it. Or find my way back.

> sunset over the sea
> I remember when my mother
> ran faster than me

HARICOTS VERTS WITH GARLIC BUTTER GLAZE

Apart from runner beans, the ones with the red hearts inside the green pod, or at least they were red until you cooked them, Dad also grew dwarf beans, but they weren't as dramatic as the runners. They (obviously, by virtue of their name) didn't grow as tall, and I couldn't lose myself in a tunnel of bristly leaves and sunlight. Picking them was more chore than adventure. So this recipe is my apology to dwarf beans, or Haricots Verts: you have my complete attention now.

What you need:
- green beans, butter, oil, 1 or 2 garlic cloves

What you do:
- Snip the tops off the beans, and the curly tails too if you don't like them
- Drop them into lightly salted boiling water for 5 to 8 minutes, until they're cooked but still have some bite. You don't want mushy beans
- Melt a knob of butter and a tablespoon of olive oil in a deep pan and add some finely chopped garlic. Swish it around over a low heat for about a minute or so until it's soft. You don't want burnt garlic
- Drain the beans and toss them in the hot garlic mix until they are glistening and steamy. You want glistening
- Serve them with anything. Or eat them on their own. Or add finely sliced salami or chorizo and shavings of parmesan for something fatter and more filling. You want them

Hungry Writing Prompts 316 - 322

Write about a vegetable garden.

Write about the smell of summer.

Write about something you made at school.

Write about what echoes to you from the past.

Write about hope.

Write about buying a new pair of shoes.

Write about running.

Eating with the Dead

I can't remember exactly when I wrote these 'instructions' for my funeral but although it was more than a decade before I started the hungry writer blog you'll notice that food plays a pretty central part!

Given a choice

I'd like a sunny day, a party
in the garden, a wooden table laid
with a white cloth. A bowl of cherries
for a stone spitting competition. Veuve Clicquot
served in uncut glass, brandied sugar cubes
and people dancing barefoot in the long grass.

If it's cold and rainy, rent an old manor house
surrounded by fields. Roast chickens and eat them
with your hands, crusty bread. Ripe peaches.
Drink Grand Marnier on ice in a wood-panelled lounge,
a fierce fire in front of your feet. Fall asleep
between fat feathered duvets and crisp white
sheets.

If it's only you, my love, tip what remains of me
into the sea, then cook our favourite meal –
prawns in garlic, fillet steak, sweet chips.
Open the wine with the Picasso label
we've been meaning to drink. Talk
to someone you love on the phone.

If I'm alone, I choose a mountain
of slate and gorse and will slowly slip
between the seams of stone, listening
to the cries of sheep, the rain coming home.

I keep it with my will, and while I like to hope the people who find
it will carry out, as far as possible, my wishes, it really won't matter
to me by that time. After all, funerals are for the living: people need
to do whatever helps them say goodbye and grieve.

But in case anyone reading this is likely to be around at the time
of my demise: the Veuve Clicquot (Brut) is not negotiable.

I never went to the funeral of the woman who gave me the following recipe for pears poached in red wine.

She was the girlfriend, and then wife, of an entertainments agent
who used to book Tony for gigs around the South East when he was
a professional entertainer. I went to their wedding, had dinner at
their house in Sussex a few times. She collected old porcelain dolls,
and a whole clan of them used to stare out of a glass fronted cupboard in the dining room while we ate. She kept a horse. She wore
long clothes: skirts and cardigans that seemed to wrap her like blankets. She came to one of our fancy dress parties as Charlie Chaplin
and strutted like a penguin and twirled her cane all night with an
exuberance I'd never seen when she was being herself. Once, when
they came to lunch, Tony made her a flambéed peach for dessert in
place of the bananas he was making for everyone else. Her husband
peered into the frying pan and exclaimed in complete innocence,
'Oh, darling, your peach is wrinkled!' and Tony and I howled with
school-yard laughter, hanging onto the edge of the kitchen cabinets
like a couple of wet tea-towels.

She wasn't my friend. And I hadn't seen her for years when I
heard she'd died. But I think of her every time I make these pears:

her long black hair, her pale skin and small mouth, her dark clothes, a little like the Victorian dolls she collected. And that's it. I'd be lying if I said there was an emotional connection. Except perhaps a subliminal gratitude for the recipe because the pears are so good and turn out well every time I make them. And it makes me think about the idea that the dead are always with us in some way. And how stories keep on growing.

Is someone I've served these pears to thinking about me? If so, please imagine me in a pretty dress, a little suntanned. Let me be laughing.

LESLEY'S PEARS POACHED IN RED WINE

What you need:
- ☐ 5 ounces of sugar
- ☐ 1/4 pint of red wine
- ☐ 1/4 pint of water
- ☐ 1 inch of cinnamon stick
- ☐ 6 dessert pears (I tend to use Conference)
- ☐ 1 teaspoon of arrowroot, maybe
- ☐ flaked almonds

(Because I like loads of syrup I double the amounts of sugar, wine, water and cinnamon when I make it. Minimum-syrup people should stick to the original quantities.)

What you do:
- ☐ In a large pan, over a low heat, melt the sugar in the wine and water, with the cinnamon stick, then boil for 15 minutes
- ☐ In the meantime, peel the pears, leaving the stalks on for decoration, and cut a slice off the bottom of each one if you want to serve them standing up in a bowl like sweet fruity soldiers. But they look just as nice lying down, like 6 in a bed (or 5 in this case)
- ☐ Reduce the syrup to a simmer, slip the pears in and spoon the syrup over them. I turn them, gently, every 10 minutes for about 40 to 50 minutes to make sure they're cooked all the way through. You can always pierce them with a cocktail stick (somewhere unnoticeable) to check. But I'd go for 10 minutes more rather than take the chance on underdone. You want yielding not crunchy
- ☐ By this time the syrup is usually syrupy enough so I don't need to thicken it with the arrowroot. If you do then take the pears out first, mix the arrowroot into a little bit of cold water, add it to the bubbling syrup and stir well
- ☐ You can decorate them with a good handful of toasted flaked almonds: throw them in a non-stick frying pan and keep stirring over a medium heat for a minute or so. Don't worry about getting them brown all over. And don't walk away – they burn quickly. Trust me

Hungry Writing Prompts 323 – 329

Write about the day of your death.

Write about grieving.

Write about someone you don't know

Write about an old doll.

Write about dressing up.

Write about the dead who are always with you.

Write about lying.

Hearth Food: Heart Food
In memory of Martin James 1905 – 1975

My maternal grandfather, *Dadcu* in Welsh, or *D'cu* (phonetically, 'duhkey') as we used to call him, Martin James, had two dietary practices that no one else in my life, then or since, has repeated. He used to swallow a raw egg in the mornings, the yolk bobbing about in its albumen as he tipped the glass towards his mouth. I imagined the yellow dome breaking in his throat as he swallowed. And he sliced cheddar cheese into a glass dish and placed it in front of the open coal fire to melt. Then he spooned it onto fresh, hand-cut white bread. I remember tasting the melted cheese. I remember the pull and slip of it against the spoon, like soft toffee. I kept a safe distance from any involvement with

the raw egg.

It didn't occur to me that *D'cu*'s melted cheese was a traditional Welsh dish. *Caws pobi*: roasted or baked cheese. And some people might wonder what the difference is between melted cheese spooned onto bread from a dish and cheese melted on toast under the grill. But I think you'll have to make some to appreciate it. I suppose, primarily, cooking something at an open hearth pre-dates grilling by some considerable time, so there's an historical element that affects us when we cook this way. But there really is something about the taste and texture and contrast of temperatures that you just don't get with cheese on toast. And perhaps the idea of sitting in front of a real fire, and watching your food cook, taps into a primitive satisfaction and a time when the world rolled along at a slower pace. And, of course, for me, it connects me to my *D'cu* too, a slight man with a big heart who was old before his time, like so many men of his generation who lost their youth and health to Welsh tinplate works and coal mines.

In Bobby Freeman's *First Catch Your Peacock*, a cross between a cookery book and a history book about the food of Wales, from earliest times right up to the 20th century, she talks about the Welsh early passion for *caws pobi*, the forerunner of the internationally known Welsh Rarebit and traces references back to medieval and Tudor times. But, interestingly, the cheese best suited to 'roasting' was a hard cheese like English Cheddar, and not the softer cheeses then being made in Wales, a result of the soil's acidity, although cheese made from ewe's milk, like the Spanish Manchego was, she assumes, a good alternative.

With the idea of *pobi*-ying some *caws* I call for French bread at the tiny Spar attached to our local garage here in Kent, whose lovely proprietors stock local products and speciality ones from all over the British Isles. I spot a wheel of Ginger Spice, one of the flavoured cheddars made by the Snowdonia Cheese Company. And Snowdon, the highest peak in Wales, is about as Welsh as you can get! When I get home I slice this and some Cornish cheddar into a nonstick pan and put it on the top of our wood-burning stove, not expecting the heat of its metal jacket to set it sizzling at quite an alarming rate. In less than a minute they had melted to within memories of themselves and started to burn.

But clouds and silver linings and all that … once I'd spooned off what I could and slathered it onto hunks of fresh bread (pause here for some enjoyable chewing…) I was left with a cooling crispy cheese crust that lifted off the pan like a savoury veil. Parmesan crisps? Forget about them: *creision* (crisps) *caws pobi* are the future.

D'cu melted his cheese more slowly, away from the fire's direct heat. Too slowly from a kid's perspective when having to wait for anything makes you fidget like a Mexican jumping bean. But I'm also guessing his generation wouldn't have been anywhere near as impatient as we are today when we so easily rankle at a slow internet speed, traffic jams, queues at banks or supermarkets.

I need to tackle *caws pobi* again: at a different pace. In a thicker oven-proof dish for a start. Or maybe I could prop it up on a few logs in front of the wood-burner's open door where I can sit and watch the flames, their hypnotic flare and flicker. Food, like the memories of people we loved, still love, shouldn't be rushed.

Thanks, *D'cu. Cysgu yn dawel.* Sleep peacefully.

Hungry Writing Prompts 330 – 336

Write about an egg.

Write about a grandparent.

Write about staring into a fire.

Write about burning.

Write a story about the origin of a particular
food or recipe, fact or fiction.

Write about what makes you impatient.

Write about sleeping peacefully.

Meal for One

This is not say that I don't love you, but now I have waved you off to London for the evening and I have cleaned the kitchen floor, showered and changed, lit the wood-burning stove to

counter the chill of the late April air, I am just so happy to be here alone in our yellow kitchen, slicing the buttered and peppered Jersey Royals left over from last night's dinner, chopping a small red onion, snipping chives into confetti, whisking two eggs and sipping cold white wine.

It seems that omelettes were made for solitude, made for one. They slip out of their pans and onto a single plate. They yield to a fork held in one hand. And this one asks to be eaten here and now, after I've sliced it into four and layered it beside a small nest of rocket drizzled with oil, while I'm still standing at the kitchen bar. No etiquette of table or table-mat, no knife, no napkin. Not a single spoken word.

This is not to say that I don't love you, but the last slice I thought I'd never eat, the slice too far, the one I thought I'd keep for you when you came home, the snack you might be thinking of when you opened the door, the one I dressed with a spear of chive just for you, has also gone. This was always meant to be a meal for one.

Hungry Writing Prompts 337 - 343

Write about loving someone.

Write about being alone.

Write about chopping vegetables.

Write about eating with your hands.

Write about changing your mind.

Write about selfishness.

Write about not loving someone.

An Interlude for Chips

Fat

Skinny women order his fish
fried in low-cholesterol oil,
batter as crisp and sheer as glass.

He teases them about goose-fat,
the slip of it, how it dimples
under fingertips, at the right point
of tenderness how it gives
to the tip of a tongue.

He dreams of women
whose flesh parts for him
like lard – their overlap, the spill
and pleat of them, his hands skating
over their suety gleam, their excess
rejoicing under his palms.

From *Learning How to Fall* (Parthian 2005)

Hungry Writing Prompts 344 – 350

Write about skinny women.

Write about glass.

Write about a point of tenderness.

Write about a man's dreams.

Write about fleshy women.

Write a list of things to rejoice over.

Write about chips.

Sweet Life

I'm trying to remember where my school tuck shop was. The sprawling Sandfields Comprehensive School in South Wales was divided into Lower, Middle and Upper sections of red brick buildings, each with their own assembly halls. I'm pretty sure it occupied a small room at the end of an L-shaped covered walkway behind the Lower School Hall, at the edge of a kind of no-man's land yard that joined all three areas of the school but didn't seem to belong to any particular one.

But I can't see beyond the Tuck Shop's split door, or was it a slide-open window? I can suggest a list of chocolate bars and packets of crisps from the late 1960s and early 1970s that might have nudged up against each other on the shelves but I have no memory of handing over money for a Milky Way (1935), or a Wagon Wheel (1948), or a packet of the still excitingly novel, (well, as exciting and novel as reconstituted potato gets), Cheese Quavers (1968).

The dates above are courtesy of Steve Berry's and Phil Norman's *The Great British Tuck Shop*, an encyclopaedic and entertaining memory-stirring read through all things sweet and savoury from a time when we didn't even know how to spell obesity or were familiar with type 2 diabetes.

Maybe I did buy one or two things at the school tuck shop but my strongest memory of sweet buying was closer to home, from a little flat-roofed shop at the end of Aberafan Beach's promenade, a street away from our house. Recite with me now: Black Jacks, Fruit Salads, Rainbow Drops, White Mice, Pink Shrimps, Flying Saucers, Bazooka Joes. Sweets we chose in straight and mixed pairs, triplets and quartets, according to the amount of solidly reliable brass pennies in our pockets. Pennies that betrayed us after 1971 with the decimalisation of the UK's currency when, overnight, 2.4 old pennies were now only worth 1 new one and the Black Jack count fell simultaneously.

The Great British Tuck Shop is probably best reserved for reading alone and in private, because of the risk of alarming anyone nearby when you yelp, 'Oh Aztec!' Or, 'Caramac!' And, 'Curly Wurly!' Or, perhaps even more worryingly, 'Raspberry Ruffles,' with a long and satisfying sigh.

When I say, 'Raspberry Ruffles', a whole other world rushes back to me: the worn, red velvet seats of an old cinema, the scent of perfume and cigarette smoke from the usherette as she saunters back up the aisle with her tray of ice-creams, and the heavy velvet drapes that ease themselves open across a screen that suddenly makes my eyes ache.

And then there are the people who embody my chocolate memories. My husband, Tony, is Fry's Turkish Delight (1908). My mother goes with Bournville Chocolate (1908). For my older sister there's Cadbury's Fruit and Nut (1926). My younger brother, the aforementioned laces of stiff toffee dipped in chocolate, a Curly Wurly (1970).

Me? I'm a packet of Munchies (1957). Or maybe, Rolos (1937). But what about my father? There's nothing that comes to mind. Did he like the Toffee Pennies in a Christmas tin of Quality Street (1936)? Or a sophisticated After Eight (1962)? Did Mam put a Jacob's Club (1932) – 'If you like a lot of chocolate on your biscuit join our club!' – in his box, along with his sandwiches, when he went to work? It suddenly feels important to find out.

Hungry Writing Prompts 351 - 357

Write about your first school.

Write about what you can see through an open door.

Write about a sweetshop.

Write about losing money.

Write about going to the cinema.

Write about light.

Write about someone who loves chocolate.

What Mothers Give Us

This is my mother's pressed glass cake stand, one of her wedding gifts from 1952, which she gave me some time ago. It's moved houses in Kent, and travelled with me to the South of France and back again.

In her personal essay, 'My Mother's Blue Bowl',[8] Alice Walker says, of the two bowls her mother gave her: "[My mother] taught me a lesson about letting go of possessions – easily, without emphasis or regret."

That's how I feel about my mother's gift to me.

It also feels like a part of my mother's life. For the first few years after her marriage she lived with her in-laws, renting a backroom, a bedroom and sharing the kitchen. She remembers her mother-in-law, Catherine Rees, asking if she would please teach her how to make one of her light and fluffy Victoria Sponges. 'She was so humble,' my mother still says of her. To welcome another woman into your home and your kitchen is not always an easy thing to do.

---

8   From *A Slice of Life: Contemporary Writers on Food*, ed. Bonnie Marranca, first published by Overlook Duckworth 2005.

And I remember, too, my mother making cakes when I was small – how my sister and I negotiated who would lick the bowl and who would get the spoon, eyeing up and measuring the smears of cake mixture remaining on both.

And here's a glass plate and dome I brought home from Tony's mother's house when we were clearing it out after she died in 1998. I think this must be French Luminarc or Arcoroc tempered glass-ware, as 'France' is stamped in tiny letters on the top of the lid, and it could date from anywhere between the 1960s and the 1980s.

I knew Tony's mother, Lilian, for 12 years but I cannot remember her ever using the glass domed plate. In fact, Tony can't remember it at all, so she must have bought it after he left home, in 1964. Maybe it was a one-off purchase, bought for a single occasion, a birthday or Christmas perhaps, then stored in the back of a cupboard for the rest of the time. But it still feels a part of who she was: it's big airy dome and large plate like a symbol of her generous and wonderfully transparent nature.

I use them both. For every day meals and for celebrations. They hold Welshcakes, banana bread, slices of Bara Brith, apple and sultana cake, open tarts, even cheese and grapes. They instil in me a sense of the vertical in history, not just horizontal, linear time, a sense of the years passing, but the repetition of habits and actions performed by women. And how that feels as if it starts deep in the earth beneath my feet and ascends through me and my life. And will carry on growing higher after I'm gone, not through any children of my own, but through the daughters and sons who are part of my extended family. I name them now: Ffion, Iwan, Manon, Morgan, Harri, Summer, Oliver. My history builders.

Hungry Writing Prompts 358 – 364

Write about something your mother gave you.

Write about letting go.

Write about welcoming someone into your home.

Write about something found at the back of a cupboard.

Write about generosity.

Write about what will happen after you leave this world.

Write about the children.

What Matters in the Here and Now: Food and Grace

Last night's here and now was an experiment with *Pissaladière*, a *niçoise* kind of open tart, or flat bread, filled or topped with caramelised onions, anchovies and black olives. We've invited our neighbours in for a New Year's glass or two of champagne and nibbles and I'm playing around with canapé ideas – the usual meat, fish, and vegetarian presentation. I wanted to see if the topping would hold up cooked on a sheet of puff pastry then cut into small squares. It does. But it won't. It feels more like a 'chomp on that with a glass of rustic red wine' kind of snack than a 'savour this with a glass of champagne' one.

To be honest, I'm fretting unnecessarily about this event, trying too hard to come up with little plates of food to welcome people into our home. I'm not sure why. Maybe it's a side-effect of lingering jet lag after flying back from Florida a couple of days ago. Maybe I'm focusing too much on wanting to impress people, some of whom I hardly know. A 'look at my perfectly original *amuse-bouches*, people!' approach, which really isn't the way I normally think about food and feeding people at all.

I recently bought Tamar Adler's lyrical and meditative *An Everlasting Meal: Cooking with Economy and Grace*, a book that is far more than a cookbook or a book about how we live and eat, but has so much to say about both, and more. I read it while sitting on a beach in Florida and so many times I had to close the book and close my eyes and let myself absorb the poetry of her words and insights. I know when a book is about to take up permanent residence in my life when I start scribbling notes in the margins and underlining words I want to remember. This is a book for writers who love food. 'Capers are as odd and wild as birds' (p.136). Yes, they are!

And now I'm remembering what she says on p.215:

> …the simple, blessed fact is that no one ever comes to dinner for what you're cooking. We come for the opportunity to look up from our plates and say 'thank you'. It is for recognition of our common hungers that we come when we are asked.

Now, some champagne and a few mouthfuls of savouriness are not dinner. There's no table sharing involved. But our get-together is about companionship, about living in the same lane, about what we have in common and about the differences we accept in each other.

And now I start to think about food as tenderness, as an ordinary but sincere smile, as good wishes for the now and what's to come, as the grace in the title of Tamar Adler's book. That's a start. I can go forward from here. And maybe the *Pissaladière*[9] will find a place.

Go forward with grace too – from the here and now and into whatever the future brings for you.

---

9 You'll find Tamar Adler's guidelines for making this on pages 147 to 149 of her book although there are hundreds of recipes for it on-line. But she is the only cook I've ever read who really understands the patience involved in caramelising onions. Do not believe anyone else who says 20 minutes, even half an hour, is enough. Prepare yourself to engage with them for an hour. 'Golden jam', she says. Yes.

Hungry Writing Prompt 365

Write about the grace in your life.

Hungry Reading: A Bibliography

Food and Life

Adler, Tamar, *An Everlasting Meal: Cooking with Economy and Grace* (Scribner, 2011)

Allende, Isabel, *Aphrodite, The Love of Food and the Food of Love* (Flamingo, 1998)

Barnes, Julian, *The Pedant in the Kitchen* (Atlantic Books, 2003)

Beeton, Isabella, *Mrs Beeton's Book of Household Management* (New Edition, Ward Lock & Co., 1912)

Berry, Steve & Norman, Phil, *The Great British Tuck Shop* (Kindle edition, The Friday Project, 2012)

Bryson, Bill, *At Home* (Black Swan, 2010)

Colón, Suzan, *Cherries in Winter: My Family's Recipe for Hope in Hard Times* (Doubleday, 2009)

Colwin, Laurie, *Home Cooking* (Fig Tree, Penguin Books, 2012) and *More Home Cooking* (Harper Perennial, 1995)

Dahl, Sophie, *Miss Dahl's Voluptuous Delights* (Harper Collins, 2010)

Dundas, Philip, *Cooking Without Recipes* (Spring Hill, 2011)

Esquivel, Laura, *Between Two Fires: Intimate Writings on Life, Food, & Flavour* (Crown Publishers, NY, USA, 2009)

Fisher, M.F.K., *The Art of Eating* (Wiley Publishing, 2004)

Fisher, M.F.K., *With Bold Knife and Fork* (Counterpoint, Berkley CA, USA, 2002)

Freeman, Bobby, *First Catch Your Peacock* (Y Lolfa, 1996)

Hughes, Holly, *Best Food Writing 2010, 2011 & 2012* (Da Capo Press)

Lebovitz, David, *The Sweet Life in Paris* (Broadway Books, NY, 2009)

Maisto, Michelle, *The Gastronomy of Marriage: A Memoir of Food and Love* (Random House, 2009)

Marranca, Bobby (ed.), *A Slice of Life: Contemporary Writers on Food* (Overlook Duckworth, 2005)

Newton, Judith, *Tasting Home: Coming of Age in the Kitchen* (She Writes Press, Berkley, CA, USA, 2013)

Pollan, Michael, *Food Rules: An Eater's Manual* (Penguin, 2010)

Slater, Nigel, *Eating for England* (Harper Perennial, 2007)

Slater, Nigel, *Toast: the Story of a Boy's Hunger* (Fourth Estate, 2003)

Spencer, Colin, *British Food* (Grub Street, London, 2011)

Toklas, Alice B., *The Alice B Toklas Cookbook* (Serif, London, 1994)

Various, *In My Mother's Kitchen: Writers on Love, Cooking, and Family* (Chamberlain Bros, Penguin, 2006)

Wilson, Bee, *Consider the Fork: A History of How We Cook and Eat* (Basic Books, 2013)

Wizenberg, Molly, *A Homemade Life: Stories and Recipes from My Kitchen Table* (Simon & Schuster, 2013)

Fiction

Bender, Aimee, *The Particular Sadness of Lemon Cake* (Windmill Books, 2011)

Crace, Jim, *The Devil's Larder* (Viking, 2001)

Kolpen, Jana, *The Secrets of Pistoulet* (Stewart, Tabori & Chang, NY, 1996)

Philosophy and Science

Baggini, Julian, *The Virtues of the Table: How to Eat and Think* (Granta Books, 2014)

Smith, Robert Rowland, *Breakfast with Socrates* (Profile Books, 2010)

Standage, Tom, *An Edible History of Humanity* (Atlantic Books, 2009)

Wrangham, Richard, *Catching Fire: How Cooking Made Us Human* (Profile Books, 2010)

Poetry

Adolph, Andrea, Vallis, Donald L. & Walker, Anne F., *Bite to Eat Place: An Anthology of Contemporary Food Poetry and Poetic Prose* (Redwood Coast Press, Oakland, CA, USA, 1995)

Krawiec, Richard (ed.), *The Sound of Poets Cooking* (Jacar Press, Durham, NC, USA, 2009)

Stowell, Phyllis & Foster, Jeanne (eds), *Appetite: Food as Metaphor: An Anthology of Women Poets* (BOA Editions, Rochester, NY, USA, 2002)

Washington, Peter, (ed.), *Eat, Drink, and be Merry: Poems About Food and Drink* (Everyman's Library, Alfred A. Knopf, NY, USA, 2003)

Writing

Jacob, Diane, *Will Write for Food: The Complete Guide to Writing Cookbooks, Blogs, Reviews, Memoir and More* (Da Capo, 2010)

Thomas, Abigail, *Thinking About Memoir* (Sterling Publishing New York & London, 2008)

Ideas for Readers, Writers and Writing Groups

L et me just say: the Hungry Writing Prompts aren't compulso-
ry. I'm not metaphorically standing behind you and breathing
my expectations into your neck! Although, I imagine that your
memory and imagination have been jolted by scene and sound, by
taste and scent, as you've read some of the stories. If you haven't
written before you might like to think about giving it a go. Buy
a plain notebook – anything too fancy will place pressure on you
to write exquisitely from the let-go and first scribblings and drafts
don't have to be beautifully formed. They only have to be laid down
quietly on the page in whatever shape they arrive.

And remember, you don't have to share a word with anyone
else, not until you choose to. Writing doesn't have to be a commu-
nal activity. We write, in the first instance, for ourselves, to mine
our memories and imaginations, to find out what we think and feel
about things.

And don't be too quick to judge your writing, while you're doing it or when you first read back over it. Our internal critics are a
snippy lot, disposed to putting us down rather than building us up
when we start to explore our creativity. Ignore the voices that tell
you your words aren't good enough or uninteresting and keep on
writing.

If writing becomes a regular part of your life, and you decide to
develop some of your ideas into longer stories or poems and share
them with others, that's when you can invite your critical mind
to the table. She'll be far more objective and useful to you when
there's some distance between the original writing time and any
editing choices.

If you're already a practising writer, you might decide to use the
prompts in the privacy of your own notebook, making personal
journeys into your past or into the lives of characters in invented
worlds.

If you belong to a writers' group there's the option to use a
prompt as a timed spontaneous writing exercise then share each
other's explorations in a 'read-around'. It never fails to amaze me

how the same starting point can fragment into so many diverse directions from the pens of different people.

The results of spontaneous writing can be raw, exciting or hesitant. We share them in an atmosphere of trust and any critical commentary at this stage can be wounding and destructive. But if we want to improve our craft as writers then we do need to expose our words to constructive criticism at some point. This is when a structured workshop can be so beneficial, with each writer given time to share or read her work and receive the considered feedback of her peers.

I've directed this kind of workshop with private groups and within more formal settings in Further and Higher Education but my guidelines remain more or less the same. I believe they help create an atmosphere of respect and encourage self-discipline. That's not to say following them will always make listening to your work being discussed an easy experience! We are just too inconveniently human not to be annoyed, irritated or disappointed when someone doesn't understand us. But persevere among the people who you know, deep down, care about you and your writing, who want to see you improve, for your words to have resonance and meaning.

GUIDELINES FOR A STRUCTURED WORKSHOP

This kind of workshop is an opportunity to receive feedback on your own work and to offer feedback to other members of your group. If the work is short you can distribute copies and read it out loud at your meeting. Longer pieces benefit from being circulated beforehand and read in advance. Write brief comments on each manuscript as you read it. It's also a good idea to elect a 'chairperson' for the workshop, so they can keep an eye on timekeeping and make sure the discussions remain on track and focused.

WHEN YOUR WORK IS BEING DISCUSSED

Do not:
- introduce it by saying how bad, unfinished, trivial or unworthy

it is.

- explain the reasons why you wrote it or say where and how you wrote it, e.g. on the train on my way to see my sister!

- say anything at all until the group have finished commenting for the allotted amount of time and you're invited to speak. This means you stay silent throughout the critique.

- defend and explain your writing when you are invited to speak. Of course point out if something has been completely misunderstood but consider that the difficulty may lie with your language and/or structure. Sometimes the best response is to thank people for their input and go home and think about what's been said or suggested (with a large glass of wine!)

But do:

+ ask briefly beforehand for the specific feedback you would like, e.g. about the title, or the dialogue or any character.

+ make notes on your copy as people talk, even if you don't immediately agree with what they say.

WHEN SOMEONE ELSE'S WORK IS BEING DISCUSSED

Do Not:
- criticise in a way that will make the writer feel stupid or insulted. Think about how you'd feel listening to comments on your writing.

- make sweeping judgements, e.g. 'this is good/bad', but try and give personal specific responses using 'I', e.g. 'I was moved by … I was confused on page 2 …'

- tell stories from your own experience that the work in question reminds you of. This is not your time.

- try to make major changes or impose your own view. Your job is to help the writer convey his or her own view more clearly.

- expound on a point that has already been clearly made but acknowledge it and say you agree.

But Do:

+ try to believe in the possibilities of each piece.

+ articulate your response as clearly as you can. It is not enough to simply feel something. Good critique depends on making conscious and articulating your responses to the words you read.

+ tell the author what you liked, what moved you, what you can still see or feel, what you remember most clearly.

+ tell them where you lost attention or were confused.

+ write notes on your copy of their work, and give it to them. This is particularly suitable for noting small errors in grammar, punctuation and spelling which do not need to be discussed during a workshop.

That's a lot to absorb, so don't beat yourself up if you find yourself speaking when you should be silent, or repeating a point that's already been made. Writing is a process. And we, as writers, are part of that process. We grow. We sometimes fall. But then we rise.

Hungry Writing Prompts

Hungry Writing Prompts 1 - 7
Write about walking away from home.
Write about what you can see on the horizon.
Write about slowing down.
Write about summer fruits.
Write about waiting.
Write about someone who cares.
Write about doing something well.

Hungry Writing Prompts 8 - 14
Write about drinking in a hotel bar.
Write about running after someone.
Write about being misunderstood.
Write about doing something without permission.
Write about a time when *Les Anglais ont debarqué*.
Write about a garden.
Write about the colour yellow.

Hungry Writing Prompts 15 - 21
Write about a baby.
Write about your responsibilities.
Write about feeling vulnerable.
Write about your reflection in the mirror.
Write about your different roles and identities.
Write about what expands your life.
Write about a best friend.

Hungry Writing Prompts 22 - 28
Write about opening a cupboard door.
Write about a room that has a particular smell.
Write about what's changed.
Write about ice.
Write about something given with love.
Write about your heart.
Write about not eating.

Hungry Writing Prompts 29 - 35
Write about something your father said.
Write about waving goodbye.
Write about looking out of a train window.
Write about snow.
Write about a proposal of marriage.
Write about something done out of necessity.
Write about dancing.

Hungry Writing Prompts 36 – 42
Write about behaving badly.
Write about protecting yourself.
Write about a film that made you cry.
Write an apology to someone you love.
Write about your mistakes.
Write about what's easy.
Write about a dish you would serve to say sorry.
Hungry Writing Prompts 43 – 49
Write about a holiday.
Write about forgetting something.
Write about hope.
Write about a thunderstorm.
Write about eating on a beach.
Write about the absolutely familiar.
Write about what hurts you.
Hungry Writing Prompts 50 – 56
Write about being in an airport.
Write about the first taste of something.
Write about a 'sad reality'.
Write about the voice of someone you cannot see.
Write about a time when you judged someone.
Write about the colour of your skin.
Write about politeness.
Hungry Writing Prompts 57 – 63
Write about something you cried over as a child.
Write about failure.
Write about a conversation between two people in a street.
Write about an accident.
Write about what is beautiful for you.
Write about being alone.
Write about what you miss.
Hungry Writing Prompts 64 – 70
Write about a summer before things changed.
Write about resistance.
Write about trying something new.
Write about keeping someone safe.
Write about what god is for you.
Write about not getting what you want.
Write about the emotional aspect of saying goodbye.
Hungry Writing Prompts 71 – 77
Write about opening a box.
Write about a buying a present.

Write about a joke that's not funny.
Write about loving ugliness.
Write about dust.
Write about your muse.
Write about a bad time.

Hungry Writing Prompts 78 – 84

Write about what you can't remember.
Write about the street you lived on as a child.
Write about the journey to or home from school.
Write about a derelict house.
Write about what 'difference' means to you.
Write about virtues and flaws.
Write about what you remember.

Hungry Writing Prompts 85 – 91

Write about dressing up.
Write about singing.
Write about boys at school.
Write about something you believed to be true but later turned out
to be false.
Write about food that reminds you of home.
Write about plumpness.
Write about your mother's hands.

Hungry Writing Prompts 92 – 98

Write about the last person to leave.
Write about packing a suitcase.
Write about what's left over.
Write about picking fruit from a tree.
Write about a picnic.
Write about climbing the stairs.
Write about a door opening.

Hungry Writing Prompts 99 – 105

Write about forgetting.
Write about a moment of tension.
Write about happy companionship.
Write about a first date.
Write about a formal event or occasion.
Write about air.
Write about saying, 'Thank you'.

Hungry Writing Prompts 106 – 112

Write about a memory that makes you feel uncomfortable.
Write about applying pressure.
Write about exclusion.
Write about being curious.

Write about the girl next door.
Write about a lesson learned.
Write about kindness.

Hungry Writing Prompts 113 - 119
Write about something that changes over time: a person, a relationship, a journey.
Write about dreaming.
Write about a teacher you had at school.
Write about not wanting something to be true.
Write about flight.
Write about firm ground.
Write about what you are experiencing right now, in this moment.

Hungry Writing Prompts 120 - 126
Write about one item of food you couldn't do without.
Write about cruelty.
Write about 'a last supper'.
Write about watching someone eat.
Write about bones.
Write about what you're unsure of.
Write about something you don't like in yourself.

Hungry Writing Prompts 127 - 133
Write about an empty house.
Write about a child's drawing.
Write about breathing.
Write about filling the silence.
Write about belonging to someone or something.
Write about sisters.
Write about the smell of grass.

Hungry Writing Prompts 134 - 140
Write about something that disappeared.
Write about a man who came to your house.
Write about making a sandwich.
Write about drunkenness.
Write about throwing something across a room.
Write about being ashamed.
Write about someone's smile.

Hungry Writing Prompts 141 - 147
Write about a time you said something then wished you could take it back.
Write about blindness.
Write about the signs of danger.
Write about a dark street.
Write about someone else's children.

Write about a rare thing.
Write about falling.

Hungry Writing Prompts 148 – 154

Write about old women.
Write about reflections in water.
Write about visiting a museum.
Write about doing whatever you want to do.
Write about a blanket on the grass.
Write about getting older.
Write about regret.

Hungry Writing Prompts 155 – 161

Write about going to the cinema.
Write about the first sip of champagne.
Write about a childhood Christmas.
Write about an adult Christmas.
Write about something a child told you.
Write about a ritual, something you repeat during the year or from year to year.
Write about James Bond.

Hungry Writing Prompts 162 – 168

Write about desperation.
Write about refusing to do what you're told.
Write about what kills us.
Write about the longing for something.
Write about take-away food.
Write about what's right in the world.
Write positively about someone or something you doubt.

Hungry Writing Prompts 169 – 175

Write about a secret.
Write about someone who lied to you.
Write about a threat.
Write about the proof of love.
Write about the person you used to be.
Write about feeling sorry for yourself.
Write about something that takes time.

Hungry Writing Prompts 176 – 182

Write about what you love to eat.
Write about the warmth of the sun.
Write about an afterlife.
Write about gifts.
Write about something you really want to say to a person in your life.
Write about a death in the family.
Write about a wake.

Hungry Writing Prompts 183 - 189
Write about someone leaving.
Write about driving towards the coast.
Write about shadows.
Write about playing games.
Write about blackberry picking.
Write about a long distance telephone call.
Write about the people who make you whole.

Hungry Writing Prompts 190 - 196
Write about a street you know well.
Write about being naked.
Write the story that precedes a familiar photograph.
Write about being ignored.
Write about a sea breeze.
Write about buttons.
Write about why you live the way you do.

Hungry Writing Prompts 197 - 203
Write about beach-combing.
Write about something you bought on holiday.
Write about taking off your clothes.
Write about bubbles.
Write an obituary for the death of Romance.
Write about dryness.
Write about someone who is high-maintenance.

Hungry Writing Prompts 204 - 210
Write about a tea party.
Write about sweetness.
Write about a wedding present.
Write about Sunday morning.
Write about something your mother made.
Write about someone who needs rescuing.
Write about loyalty.

Hungry Writing Prompts 211 - 217
Write about riding a bike.
Write about soft food.
Write about a funeral.
Write about the songs that remind you of people in your life.
Write about someone who takes offence.
Write about a birthday cake.
Write about burying something.

Hungry Writing Prompts 218 - 224
Write about the sound of bees.
Write about cold weather.

Write about disappearing.

Write about perfection.

Write about what you will do in the years you have left to live

Write about something that happened 30 years ago.

Write about delicacy.

Hungry Writing Prompts 225 – 231

Write about something quintessentially British.

Write about a conversation in a particular room.

Write about a family portrait.

Write about Christmas morning.

Write about searching.

Write about an anniversary.

Write about the business of everyday living.

Hungry Writing Prompts 232 – 238

Write about sadness.

Write about food that makes you happy.

Write about sleep.

Write about the things your parents never had.

Write about someone eating cake in a coffee shop.

Write about crying in a public place.

Write about hardness.

Hungry Writing Prompts 239 – 245

Write about a hotel breakfast.

Write about the things that unsettle you.

Write about a battle.

Write about someone's morals.

Write about being grumpy.

Write about rules, what you will and will not do.

Write about laying a table.

Hungry Writing Prompts 246 – 252

Write about the sound of rain.

Write about the scent of bed linen.

Write about your father.

Write about cats.

Write about something glimpsed on the horizon.

Write about sand.

Write about the things that remind you of love.

Hungry Writing Prompts 253 – 259

Write about something hot.

Write about a bargain.

Write about the view from your window.

Write about mist or fog.

Write about your 'furthest' memory.

Write about what you find at the bottom of a garden.
Write about damp skin.

Hungry Writing Prompts 260 – 266

Write about losing a friend.
Write about drowning.
Write about the early morning.
Write about poison.
Write about melting away.
Write about saving yourself.
Write about a lesson learned.

Hungry Writing Prompts 267 – 273

Write about what's sure in life.
Write about the beginning of a conversation.
Write about a gift received in the post.
Write about an instantaneous connection with someone or something.
Write about a child laughing.
Write about a memorable meal in another country.
Write about something that can't be measured.

Hungry Writing Prompts 274 – 280

Write about something that glitters.
Write about a memory you only partially remember and invent the rest.
Write about a spider's web.
Write about your favourite character from a fairy tale.
Write about what gets in the way of joy.
Write about a new day.
Write about having no words.

Hungry Writing Prompts 281 – 287

Write about being the only person in a room.
Write about clouds.
Write about a loaf of bread.
Write about a carnival or fairground.
Write about a flood.
Write about a grey day.
Write about a heart that's been soured.

Hungry Writing Prompts 288 – 294

Write about meeting someone for the first time.
Write about persistence.
Write about the beginning of yourself.
Write about praying.
Write about a knife.
Write about being hungry.

Write about crumbs.

Hungry Writing Prompts 295 - 301

Write about something you used to believe but don't anymore.

Write about being dared to do something.

Write about someone's last words.

Write about the map of your life.

Write about a long journey.

Write about cheese.

Write about what is good.

Hungry Writing Prompts 302 - 308

Write about yourself as a child.

Write about coming home from school.

Write about having more.

Write about breakfast.

Write about the objects you remember in your parents' house.

Write about having less.

Write about a boy and the man he becomes.

Hungry Writing Prompts 309 - 315

Write about giving something away.

Write about what's too big for you.

Write about too much sweetness.

Write about not having enough to eat.

Write about being caught in a storm.

Write about sharing.

Write about climbing a mountain.

Hungry Writing Prompts 316 - 322

Write about a vegetable garden.

Write about the smell of summer.

Write about something you made at school.

Write about what echoes to you from the past.

Write about hope.

Write about buying a new pair of shoes.

Write about running.

Hungry Writing Prompts 323 - 329

Write about the day of your death.

Write about grieving.

Write about someone you don't know

Write about an old doll.

Write about dressing up.

Write about the dead who are always with you.

Write about lying.

Hungry Writing Prompts 330 - 336

Write about an egg.

Write about a grandparent.

Write about staring into a fire.

Write about burning.

Write a story about the origin of a particular food or recipe, fact or fiction.

Write about what makes you impatient.

Write about sleeping peacefully.

Hungry Writing Prompts 337 – 343

Write about loving someone.

Write about being alone.

Write about chopping vegetables.

Write about eating with your hands.

Write about changing your mind.

Write about selfishness.

Write about not loving someone.

Hungry Writing Prompts 344 – 350

Write about skinny women.

Write about glass.

Write about a point of tenderness.

Write about a man's dreams.

Write about fleshy women.

Write a list of things to rejoice over.

Write about chips.

Hungry Writing Prompts 351 – 357

Write about your first school.

Write about what you can see through an open door.

Write about a sweetshop.

Write about losing money.

Write about going to the cinema.

Write about light.

Write about someone who loves chocolate.

Hungry Writing Prompts 358 – 364

Write about something your mother gave you.

Write about letting go.

Write about welcoming someone into your home.

Write about something found at the back of a cupboard.

Write about generosity.

Write about what will happen after you leave this world.

Write about the children.

Hungry Writing Prompt 365

Write about the grace in your life.

Acknowledgements

'Eat, Laugh, Cry, Remember' appeared in *Roots: Where Food Comes From and Where It Takes Us: A BlogHer Anthology,* edited by Stacy Morrison, Julie Ross Godar & Rita Arens (Open Road Integrated Media/BlogHer, 2013)

'Trouble' was featured on Philip Dundas' Pip's Dish website in May 2011 (http://www.pipsdish.co.uk)

A version of 'Desperate for a McDonald's' appeared in *Real Port Talbot* (Seren, 2013)

'Summer of 1963' in 'Pantry' appeared in *forgiving the rain* (Snapshot Press, 2012)

Cultured Llama Publishing
Poems | Stories | Curious Things

Cultured Llama was born in a converted stable. This creature of humble birth drank greedily from the creative source of the poets, writers, artists and musicians that visited, and soon the llama fulfilled the destiny of its given name.

Cultured Llama is a publishing house, a multi-arts events promoter and a fundraiser for charity. It aspires to quality from the first creative thought through to the finished product.

www.culturedllama.co.uk

Also published by Cultured Llama

Poetry

strange fruits by Maria C. McCarthy
Paperback; 72pp; 203×127mm; 978-0-9568921-0-2; July 2011

A Radiance by Bethany W. Pope
Paperback; 70pp; 203×127mm; 978-0-9568921-3-3; June 2012

The Strangest Thankyou by Richard Thomas
Paperback; 98pp; 203×127mm; 978-0-9568921-5-7; October 2012

The Night My Sister Went to Hollywood by Hilda Sheehan
Paperback; 82pp; 203×127mm; 978-0-9568921-8-8; March 2013

Notes from a Bright Field by Rose Cook
Paperback; 104pp; 203×127mm; 978-0-9568921-9-5; July 2013

Sounds of the Real World by Gordon Meade
Paperback; 104pp; 203×127mm; 978-0-9926485-0-3; August 2013

Digging Up Paradise: Potatoes, People and Poetry in the Garden of England by Sarah Salway
Paperback; 160pp; 203×203mm; 978-0-9926485-6-5; June 2014

The Fire in Me Now by Michael Curtis
Paperback; 98pp; 203×127mm; 978-0-9926485-4-1; September 2014

Short of Breath by Vivien Jones
Paperback; 102pp; 203×127mm; 978-0-9926485-5-8; November 2014

Cold Light of Morning by Julian Colton
Paperback; 90pp; 203×127mm; 978-0-9926485-7-2; March 2015

The Lost of Syros by Emma Timpany
Paperback; 128pp; 203×127mm; 978-0-9932119-2-8; July 2015

Automatic Writing by John Brewster
Paperback; 92pp; 203×127mm; 978-0-9926485-8-9; July 2015

Zygote Poems by Richard Thomas
Paperback; 62pp; 203×178mm; 978-0-9932119-5-0; July 2015

Les Animots: A Human Bestiary by Gordon Meade, images by Douglas Robertson
Hardback; 164pp; 203×127mm; 978-0-9926485-9-6; October 2015

Short stories

Canterbury Tales on a Cockcrow Morning by Maggie Harris
Paperback; 136pp; 203×127mm; 978-0-9568921-6-4; September 2012

As Long as it Takes by Maria C. McCarthy
Paperback; 166pp; 203×127mm; 978-0-9926485-1-0; February 2014

In Margate by Lunchtime by Maggie Harris
Paperback; 204pp; 203×127mm; 978-0-9926485-3-4; March 2015

The Lost of Syros by Emma Tympany
Paperback; 128pp; 203×127mm; 978-0-9932119-2-8; July 2015

Non-fiction

Digging Up Paradise: Potatoes, People and Poetry in the Garden of England by
Sarah Salway
Paperback; 160pp; 203×203mm; 978-0-9926485-6-5; June 2014

**Punk Rock People Management: A No-Nonsense Guide to Hiring, Inspiring
and Firing Staff** by Peter Cook
Paperback; 40pp; 229×152mm; 978-0-9932119-0-4; February 2015

Do it Yourself: A History of Music in Medway by Stephen H. Morris
Paperback; 504pp; 229×152mm; 978-0-9926485-2-7; April 2015

The Music of Business: Business Excellence Fused with Music by Peter Cook
Paperback; 318pp; 210×148mm; 978-0-9932119-1-1; May 2015

The Ecology of Everyday Things by Mark Everard
Hardback; 126pp; 216×140mm; 978-0-9932119-6-6; November 2015

Lightning Source UK Ltd.
Milton Keynes UK
UKOW07f1617260116

267129UK00004B/26/P